STAFFORDSHIRE BULL
Terrier

Dedication

To the most special people in my life, without whom I would
not be what I am now: John Fletcher, Ruth and Willis Ford, my husband Syd,
my babies Zara and Asher, Jayne Pashley and Dan-Dan! Also Arlene Fletcher,
my Mum, who I miss beyond words.

Alison Smith

Alison Smith was brought up with Bull Terriers, Staffordshire Bull Terriers
and Rottweilers. She has owned seven Staffords over the last 20 years and,
along with her husband Paul, has had some success in the show ring.
She is currently 'owned' by Fred and Betty! Alison is the Editor of the
UK's oldest canine newspaper, *Our Dogs*.

David Taylor B.V.M.S., F.R.C.V.S., F.Z.S.

David Taylor is a veterinary surgeon and author who has worked with a wide
spectrum of animal species for many years. Founder of the International Zoo
Veterinary Group, he has had patients ranging from the King of Spain's Giant
Pandas to gorillas in West Africa and killer whales with frostbite in Iceland.
He has written over 100 books on animal matters including many best-selling
dog books and seven volumes of autobiography. The latter formed the basis
for three series of the BBC television drama *One by One*. He lives in
Hertfordshire, England.

STAFFORDSHIRE BULL
Terrier

AN OWNER'S GUIDE

Alison Smith

Healthcare by
David Taylor

First published in 2009 by
Collins, an imprint of
HarperCollins Publishers
77–85 Fulham Palace Road
Hammersmith, London W6 8JB

The Collins website address is:
www.collins.co.uk

Collins is a registered trademark of HarperCollins Publishers Limited
11 10 09
6 5 4 3 2 1

A catalogue record for this book is available from the British Library.

Created by: SP Creative Design
Editor: Heather Thomas
Designer: Rolando Ugolini
Photography: Rolando Ugolini

ISBN: 978-0-00-727428-4

Printed and bound by Printing Express Ltd., Hong Kong

Acknowledgements
The Breed Standard on pages 16–17 is reproduced by kind permission of
the Kennel Club. The publishers would also like to thank the following
individuals for their help in producing the photography in this book: Lesley
McFadyen and her dogs Dot, Jack, Carey, Angel, Thyme and Roly; Clive
Gowlett and Wilson; Wendy Clewley and Marvin, Tammy, Katie, Archie and
Tia; Becca Hayter-Gare and Marmite and Boysie; Jo-Ann Essex and Clayd,
Suggs, Sumi-e, Bacon, Peppa and Poppy; and Julia Thompson and Prince.

Note: Dogs are referred to as 'he' throughout to avoid 'he'/'she' each time or
the rather impersonal 'it'. This reflects no bias towards males, and both sexes
are equally valuable and easy to train.

Contents

PART ONE

YOU AND YOUR DOG

Owning a dog is a huge responsibility but extremely rewarding. When you decide to welcome a Staffordshire Bull Terrier into your home, you have to consider not only how he will fit into your lifestyle but also what you can offer him in return. He will need regular exercise, feeding, games and companionship as well as daily care.

Chapter 1

History of the breed

The history of the dog known today as the Staffordshire Bull Terrier is, perhaps, one of the most well known histories of any breed. This loyal, people-loving dog still carries with him all the best traits that have been bred into him over the centuries to make him one of the most wonderful family pets imaginable.

Bloodsports

In the early nineteenth century, terriers of all kinds were bred for their ability to take part in what were then known as bloodsports, the two most popular being bull-baiting and cock-fighting. In the mid-1800s, bulls were brought to markets and upon by dogs. Baiting was done for two reasons: to tenderize the bull's meat and provide entertainment for the spectators, who enjoyed nothing more than watching the specially bred dogs bring down a bull. This pastime also extended to bears and other animals.

These bloodsports were very common at this time and would often take place in villages and at country fairs. The dogs would grab the bulls and be tossed around, sometimes even being hurled over a bull's head, only to be thrown back into the action by their owners.

Bred to win

The secret to a winning dog's success lay in the strength of his jaw. The ability to 'lock' his jaws onto another animal meant that, no matter how strong the opposition, the steely grip and weight of the dog would eventually tire the bull out and bring it down.

Another trait of the Staffordshire Bull Terrier was (and still is) its incredible tolerance to pain. This meant that they invariably continued to hang on, despite suffering severe injuries.

These early dogs bore no resemblance to the noble breed we are used to today. They were bred not for their pleasing looks but for what was then known as their 'gameness' – in other words, their strength and skill against animals which were over 20 times their size.

The Stafford's fearless nature, together with his in-built resolve never to quit, are still much in evidence in the breed today, although modern breeders are also careful to breed for a good, sound temperament in their dogs, so that they will make good family pets.

Opposite: The loyal Staffordshire Bull Terrier is one of the most noble looking and wonderful dogs imaginable.

Origins of the breed

The modern breed owes much of its physical attributes to the Bulldog. However, the Bulldog of the nineteenth century was a somewhat larger dog than the big-jawed and handsome one of today, with longer legs and a much more refined head, more reminiscent of the American Staffordshire Bull Terrier. The Bulldog is believed to have been crossed with several other terrier breeds in a bid to attain a dog which combined great physical strength in the head and body with an agile swiftness. This was an ideal combination for a dog who was expected to fight in small areas, often known as 'pits'. These breeds were often referred to as 'Half-and-Halfs', in a nod to the two distinct breeds that had produced them. The breed nowadays resembles both the Bulldog and the terrier, with evidence of the former still clearly seen in the head.

The breed nowadays still shows clear signs of its Bulldog and terrier ancestry. Note the famous Stafford smile, as shown below by these two handsome dogs!

The word Staffordshire relates to the part of the United Kingdom where the breed first became popular in the mid 1800s, particularly among the working classes. The Staffordshire area of the Midlands, including Birmingham, Walsall and Stoke-on-Trent, saw extensive breeding of both of this dog's forebears – Bulldogs and terriers.

The motivation was still to achieve the perfect fighting dog, and even though dog fighting was outlawed in the early 1900s, many fanciers continued to breed with the fight in mind and dogs still went head to head with each other. These clandestine fights were organized by word of mouth, culminating in a 'game' played out in someone's home, backyard or a disused building. Thus the name of the breed is a tribute both to its forefathers and place of origin, making it truly British.

Interestingly, whilst this breed's aggression towards other dogs was never doubted, it is a fact that people were often to be seen handling the dogs in the fighting pits, and yet they were rarely attacked. This is a testament to the breed's love of humans, and it is this quality that makes the Stafford such a wonderful companion to this day.

The early days
In 1888, the Bull Terrier Club of England was formed and subsequently the members published a Breed Standard – a blueprint for the breed. This Standard listed all the desirable physical and temperament points that any breeder should aspire to. All recognized

This Stafford combines the physical strength and agility which his forebears were bred for. Staffords are always happy to display their keenness for life.

breeds nowadays have their own Breed Standards, which are laid down by the Kennel Club and should be closely adhered to by breeders.

The Staffordshire Bull Terrier had to wait until the 1930s before fanciers decided to try and establish it as a breed in its own right, rather than the loose blend of bull and terrier which had existed until that time. This was due partly to the fact that the abolition of dog fighting was now being strictly enforced and 'underground fights' were regularly stopped by the police and the organizers were punished. Illegal fighting continued, however – and, sadly, still does – albeit to a much lesser degree.

Having lost their 'sport' to these new

laws, breed enthusiasts started to think about what else they could do to show off their stock to other like-minded people. One way was to follow in the footsteps of many other dog breeds and perhaps start to compete against each other, not in the pit this time but in the show ring at a dog show.

The first Standard

At this point, the Stafford, as we know it now, was clearly recognizable. By cleverly breeding like to like, a very distinct and unique-looking dog was emerging. The very first Breed Standard was written by two of the Stafford's most famous custodians and breeders, Joe Dunn and Joe Mallan. The writings were based on a dog called Jim the Dandy, which was owned by Jack Barnard. Early pictures of the breed show a dog that was taller and perhaps finer looking than the Stafford today, and possibly closer to its cousin, the Bull Terrier.

In 1935, this prototype Standard was accepted at the first meeting of the newly formed Original Staffordshire Bull Terrier Club. In June of the same year, the Kennel Club (the UK's official canine governing body) officially

Popular the world over, the Staffordshire Bull Terrier is a happy-go-lucky companion who will be eager to try everything. Some even love water and swimming.

accepted it, too, thereby opening up a whole new world for the enthusiasts of the breed – the dog show.

It is perhaps unfortunate that many lovers of the breed in the mid-1930s, including people who had bred for years to create the Stafford, felt that the sport of showing was less than ideal. For them, a dog bred primarily for fighting would lose some of this trait if he was bred instead for the show ring, where a lack of 'action' would leave him naturally less aggressive over a period of time. Indeed, many secret fights were still going on, and some dogs continued to be bred for their prowess in a fight rather than in competition against the Standard.

A year later, in 1936, the Original Staffordshire Bull Terrier Club became known as the Staffordshire Bull Terrier Club, following some complaints from the Bull Terrier Club concerning the word 'original'.

First shows and famous winners
It is widely believed that the very first appearance of the breed as an exhibit was in June 1935 at Hertfordshire Agricultural Show. The first Staffordshire Bull Terrier Club show was held two months later in August at Cradley Heath in the West Midlands. The records show that 60 dogs and bitches were entered.

Around this time the breed was expanding rapidly in numbers and was sought after both as a pet and as a show dog. Whilst its origins were still very much to the fore, its popularity in the show ring meant that it was seen by many more people, as quite often the dog shows were held in conjunction with local agricultural shows, which attracted hundreds of visitors.

Challenge Certificates (see page 88) were granted to the breed by the Kennel Club not long afterwards, and the first Stafford to be awarded this high honour was a beautiful dog called Gentleman Jim at the Birmingham National championship show, which is still held in the UK every year.

In 1936, the breed was given its own class at Crufts Dog Show, and this was won by Cross Gunns Johnson, owned by Joe Dunn. In June 1946, the Southern Counties Staffordshire Bull Terrier Club held the first championship show purely for the Stafford, and breed fanciers saw an incredible entry of 300 dogs, which was testimony again to the growth in the breed's popularity.

Other dogs worthy of note at this time were Champion Gentleman Bruce, Champion Wardonion Corniche and Champion Brindle Crescendo of Wychbury. Pictures of them show a dog that had by now become much more uniform in appearance, although still perhaps a little taller than it is now.

The breed internationally
Nowadays the breed is very popular the world over. From America to Australia, from Russia to Argentina, the Stafford is revered as a wonderful pet and successful show dog. Sadly, however, there are some countries where the breed is the target of what is known as Breed Specific Legislation (BSL). This legislation came about because of a general confusion

over the Staffordshire Bull Terrier and other breeds, namely the Pit Bull Terrier and several crosses of other breeds with the Stafford. Unfortunately, the physical similarities between these breeds can sometimes appear to be quite close to the uninitiated, although to the trained eye there are many differences.

The German government tried to ban the breed across the European Union in September 2000, but luckily the intervention of the UK Kennel Club stopped this happening. The breed was banned in Ontario, Canada, in August 2005, and several other countries are closely watching the breed known as the Pit Bull Terrier. Therefore it is important that all Stafford owners behave very responsibly to avoid their breed being placed in the same category.

The Dangerous Dogs Act

As a responsible Stafford owner, the 1991 Dangerous Dogs Act (DDA) is extremely unlikely to affect you or your dog. Owning a pedigree Stafford is perfectly acceptable in the UK. However, you must always make sure that your dog's pedigree and Kennel Club papers are available, as sometimes authorities with little expertise in the breed can confuse them with banned breeds. It is also worth bearing in mind that the Stafford is banned or under severe legal restriction in Germany, Israel and Canada. Legal restrictions can take the form of muzzling your dog in public,

Opposite: As a responsible owner, you will spend many happy hours with your well trained Stafford, walking him and playing.

This owner has total control over her Stafford, who is displaying his full attention. Never allow your new dog off the lead until you have full control over him.

having to obtain a special licence, a ban on breeding and/or selling and, possibly, even having to take out special insurance for your dog.

The problem that the DDA does pose to Stafford owners in the UK is that a Stafford may physically resemble the Pit Bull Terrier to a person who is unfamiliar with the breed, which may be confusing to the uninitiated. Never allow your dog to run wild in open spaces until you are 100 per cent sure that you have full control over him, and never encourage him to display any aggression towards people or other dogs. For more information on the Dangerous Dogs Act, see page 126.

Breed Standard

General appearance Smooth-coated, well balanced, of great strength for his size. Muscular, active and agile.

Characteristics Traditionally of indomitable courage and tenacity. Highly intelligent and affectionate, especially with children.

Temperament Bold, fearless and totally reliable.

Head and skull Short, deep through with broad skull. Very pronounced cheek muscles, distinct stop, short foreface, nose black.

Eyes Dark preferred but may bear some relation to coat colour. Round, of medium size, and set to look straight ahead. Eye rims dark.

Boldness and courage are two words that are often used to describe the breed.

Ears Rose or half pricked, not large or heavy. Full, drop or pricked ears highly undesirable.

Mouth Lips tight and clean. Jaws strong, teeth large, with a perfect, regular and complete scissor bite, i.e. upper teeth closely overlapping lower teeth and set square to the jaws.

Neck Muscular, rather short, clean in outline gradually widening towards shoulders.

Forequarters Legs straight and well boned, set rather wide apart, showing no weakness at the pasterns, from which point feet turn out a little. Shoulders well laid back with no looseness at elbow.

Body Close-coupled, with level topline, wide front, deep brisket, well sprung ribs; muscular and well defined.

Hindquarters Well muscled, hocks well let down with stifles well bent. Legs parallel when viewed from behind.
Feet Well padded, strong and of medium size. Nails black in solid coloured dogs.
Tail Medium length, low-set, tapering to a point and carried rather low. Should not curl much and may be likened to an old-fashioned pump handle.
Gait/movement Free, powerful and agile with economy of effort. Legs moving parallel when viewed from front or rear. Discernible drive from hindlegs.
Coat Smooth, short and close.
Colour Red, fawn, white, black or blue, or any one of these colours with white. Any shade of brindle or any shade of

The Stafford is a strong dog with a distinctive head and a very muscular body.

brindle with white. Black and tan or liver colour highly undesirable.
Size Desirable height at withers 35.5–40.5cm (14–16in), these heights being related to the weights. Weight: dogs: 12.7–17kg (28–38lb); bitches 11–15.4kg (24–34lb).
Faults Any departure from the foregoing points should be considered a fault and the seriousness with which the fault should be regarded should be in exact proportion to its degree.
Note Male animals should have two apparently normal testicles fully descended into the scrotum.
© The Kennel Club

The Staffordshire Bull Terrier

Body Close-coupled, with level topline, wide front, deep brisket, well sprung ribs; muscular and well defined.

Coat Smooth, short and close.

Tail Medium length, low-set, tapering to a point and carried rather low. Should not curl much and may be likened to an old-fashioned pump handle.

Hindquarters Well muscled, hocks well let down with stifles well bent. Legs parallel when viewed from behind.

Feet Well padded, strong and of medium size. Nails black in solid coloured dogs.

Ears Rose or half pricked, not large or heavy. Full, drop or pricked ears highly undesirable.

Head and skull Short, deep through with broad skull. Very pronounced cheek muscles, distinct stop, short foreface, nose black.

Eyes Dark preferred but may bear some relation to coat colour. Round, of medium size, and set to look straight ahead. Eye rims dark.

Mouth Lips tight and clean. Jaws strong, teeth large, with a perfect, regular and complete scissor bite, i.e. upper teeth closely overlapping lower teeth and set square to the jaws.

Neck Muscular, rather short, clean in outline gradually widening towards shoulders.

Forequarters Legs straight and well boned, set rather wide apart, showing no weakness at the pasterns, from which point feet turn out a little. Shoulders well laid back with no looseness at elbow.

Chapter 2

Acquiring a puppy

There is a saying amongst Stafford owners, which is that once you have owned a Stafford, you will never want to have another breed of dog. It is also fairly true to say that you don't own the breed – it owns you. Such is the extent of the mark a loving Stafford can make on your life as well as your family.

I make no apology for the amount of time you will read the word 'socialized' in this chapter. Choosing a puppy who has had the benefit of a careful breeder and early socialization is so important.

Is this the breed for you?

Before you buy a Stafford, ask yourself the following questions:
• Are you out at work all day?
• Are you a couch potato?
• Do you live in a flat or bedsit with no green space?
• Are you elderly, infirm or disabled?
• Do you have other dogs?

If you have answered 'yes' to any of the above, think carefully before choosing a Stafford as your breed. These dogs thrive on company, lots of exercise, an energetic family and plenty of room to call their own.

However, if you have taken this into consideration and feel that you can surmount any possible problems, then a Stafford may still make a wonderful companion for you.

Why choose a Stafford?

The Staffordshire Bull Terrier is a breed that is noted for its loyalty and devotion, as well as its deep affection for children; for this reason, it is also known as the Nanny Dog. The Stafford is a smooth-coated dog which makes him relatively easy to care for and, as a responsible owner, you will be rewarded with a companion who lives for his family and whose reason for being will begin and end with you.

This dog is extremely energetic and you must be aware that it is essential that you provide above-average exercise and establish a regular routine from an early age for your dog's mental and physical development – if you are a couch potato, then this breed is probably

A Stafford puppy will reward you with his fun-loving personality and deep love of humans, especially children.

not right for you. Your dog will thrive on companionship and love and is not a suitable pet if you are away from him for long periods, as this will inevitably lead to difficulty in maintaining the level-headedness required in this physically strong breed.

You must also bear in mind that this cute puppy – and they *are* adorable – will grow into a strong and powerful animal who will require a strong arm to control him and will probably remain a juvenile in his outlook and behaviour. This breed is boisterous and friendly, and age and maturity will do little to diminish this. If you feel ready for this

Make sure that you see the prospective puppies with their mother. They should always be in clean and warm surroundings and should play well together.

wonderful breed, you have taken your first step to owning a Staffordshire Bull Terrier just by buying this book.

It is important to remember that the history of the Stafford means that although he is a wonderful companion, his tolerance of other dogs is low. Good breeders will keep a number of Staffords together from puppyhood, but their potential aggression towards other dogs means that socialization from an early age is essential.

The first steps

First things first now that you have taken the decision to look for a Stafford. There are hundreds of reputable breeders of Staffordshire Bull Terriers and, initially, you will need to make contact with several and talk to them. Lists of these breeders are readily available from the Kennel Club (see page 126) or from breed clubs countrywide and they will be only too happy to give advice and point you in the right direction.

The most important thing you should remember when acquiring a puppy is that it is never a good idea to buy from certain people or places, and that the following should be avoided at all costs:

• Buying over the internet
• Buying from one of the free ad papers, particularly where the breeder has several different breeds on offer
• Buying from a person who wants to hand the puppy over anywhere other than at their home, e.g. if they offer to meet you in a car park, supermarket or motorway service station
• Buying from pet shops or supermarkets.

More often than not, the above methods are used by people who may not be accustomed to breeding correctly and they might disregard certain aspects of their dogs' welfare and health. These puppies may have had little or no early socialization, which is a recipe for trouble in a breed where this is essential.

Talking to breeders and owners

When you telephone breeders to make contact, don't be offended if they ask you more questions than you ask them.

They will be anxious to establish that their puppy is going to an environment where he will be happy, well cared for and brought up sensibly. This is a good opportunity for you to find out about anything that may be worrying you, so don't be afraid to ask, no matter how silly you think it sounds. Any good breeder will always be there to offer you help and advice and even to take back a puppy if things don't work out in his new home.

It is a good idea to spend some time talking to other Stafford owners and maybe attending dog shows where you can meet the breed. Don't just look for a local dog – you may have to venture further afield to find the right puppy for you with a good temperament so be prepared to travel several hundred miles if necessary; it will definitely be worth it. When you locate the right breeder, they may not have a suitable puppy available immediately and you might find yourself on a waiting list. If this is the case, be patient and use the time to read about the breed and prepare your home for the new arrival.

Choosing a puppy

When you have researched the breed and spoken to owners and breeders, you will be in a position to choose your puppy. Breeders often breed dogs whose temperament and conformation to the Breed Standard make them eligible as potential show dogs. If you feel that you may be interested in showing your dog, you must mention this to the breeder right at the start. They will then be able

to make sure that you have what they consider to be a 'show quality' Stafford. However, no breeder is clever enough to see into the future and therefore you must not be disappointed if your showing success does not stretch to Best in Show at Crufts!

Once you have made contact with a suitable breeder and a litter of puppies is available, you will be asked to visit the puppies at home. Be prepared to see them at about four to six weeks even though they will not be able to leave their mother until they are at least eight weeks old, or sometimes a little older.

What to look for

Always make sure that you are offered the opportunity to see the puppies with their mother. This will not offend a good breeder and will give you the extra peace of mind that they really are home-bred. You will also be able to use this visit to gauge the mother's temperament, so always look for signs of a happy and very friendly dog.

This is your chance to ascertain that the puppies' environment is a loving and suitable one. Check for things like clean bedding, fresh water, toys and space for the puppies to move around in. If the litter is being kept in a kennel, make sure that it seems warm and accessible. All these factors will indicate whether the breeder is genuine and caring, which, in turn, helps create a well socialized and healthy litter of puppies.

Opposite: This young Stafford looks a picture of health, with a shiny coat and eyes. His interest in his toy indicates a good disposition.

The puppies' coats should look shiny and healthy. It is generally agreed that a wet nose and nice clear eyes are also signs of good health. Make sure that they do not look too thin – Stafford pups should have a decent covering of coat and flesh but without looking fat. Their ears should be clean with no discharge, and the puppies should not smell unpleasant.

Do watch out for any signs of nervousness or aggression, particularly in the mother. Staffords are often said to smile, but be on the look-out for any baring of the teeth towards humans as this can often mean that the bitch has not been socialized properly. However, do bear in mind the natural maternal instinct of the new mum, who may be upset by strangers being too 'full on' with her pups. The breeder will usually be more than happy to remove a puppy from the mother for you to look at.

Take your time

You don't have to choose a puppy straight away, and if there is anything you are unhappy about, just make your excuses politely and leave. Watch the pups interact with each other and ask to visit again if wished. You may easily recognize the ones within a litter who are more dominant, aggressive or shy. You may even find that a pup will end up picking you rather than the other way round.

Things to bear in mind

The character of the Stafford is fairly equal in both the dog and the bitch. They are – and should be – feisty, fun-

loving and inquisitive. In common with puppies of any breed, however, they will require patience and time to socialize and train. This breed can tend towards dominance without some early training, making it imperative that you are prepared to donate the time and effort that are necessary to produce a really well-behaved and friendly dog who will be a credit to you.

A puppy who is integrated from an early age with other dogs is unlikely to pose a problem; often the older dogs will put him in his place from the beginning and harmony will be the order of the day. However, Staffords do not integrate easily with other Staffords (particularly when they are of the same sex), and this is something to bear in mind if you already have an older dog or bitch in your home. I have had two males live happily side by side, but I have also owned two bitches who would almost certainly have killed one another had

Watch puppies at play – you can often see which ones are going to be the bossy ones!

they been left alone together. Never just assume that Staffords will get on – it is always better to be safe than sorry.

If you do not wish to breed from your Stafford, you may wish to consider neutering. This not only prevents unwanted pregnancies in bitches but can also go some way towards preventing breast and prostate cancer. Some people believe that neutered Staffords lose some of their spark, but I have never found this to be the case, although dogs can sometimes become slightly more 'laid back' as a result.

Appearance and coat colour

Staffords come in different colours and the ones that are accepted in the breed are very varied. If you intend to show your dog, check the Breed Standard before choosing a puppy. The colour that is known as black/brindle is the most common one – this is a jet black coat on which the brindle appears, ranging from a tiny fleck to the stunning 'tiger' brindle.

Payment and papers

Good Staffords are not cheap and thus you must expect to pay handsomely for a pedigree puppy – how much will largely depend on his pedigree. The pedigree certificate should show you at least the last three generations of parentage, and champion dogs may often be highlighted in red. Ask the breeder to explain the pedigree to you if you feel unclear about it. Once you have decided that you are

happy with the breeder and want to buy a puppy, you may be asked to pay a deposit. This is usual practice and will secure the puppy for you. Later, on completion of the sale, you will be asked to pay the balance.

Rescuing a Stafford

Unfortunately, there are currently hundreds of Staffords languishing in rescue centres for a variety of reasons. They may have ended up in rescue through no fault of their own – perhaps as the result of divorce, a house move

Rescuing a Stafford can be extremely rewarding, but do think carefully about it and speak to the breed rescues beforehand.

Paperwork

Now is the time to make sure that the breeder has passed over all the relevant paperwork. You should receive the following:

- **Your dog's pedigree certificate** This should show at least the last three generations of parentage; champion dogs may often be highlighted in red
- **Your dog's registration papers** The breeder will have registered the pups with the Kennel Club. If they have registered the puppies in their name, you will have to fill in a Transfer of Ownership form and send it to the Kennel Club (with a small fee), for the dog to be registered in your name. Check with the breeder, as some register the puppy in your name to save you the trouble
- **Insurance certificate** Most puppies will come with health insurance for a free 'limited' period. Check this out with the breeder and renew when necessary
- **Vaccination diary** Your Stafford should have received his first jabs by the time you get him. Make sure you take the vaccination sheet with you – your vet will need this to fill in subsequent boosters, etc.
- **DNA profile** Some breeders have their litters DNA profiled by the Kennel Club. If this is the case, ask for the certificate.

or even the arrival of a new baby in a household. Others, sadly, are there because their early socialization was inadequate and their behaviour may have become too much for their – often well meaning – owners.

You must think carefully before you decide to rehome an adult Stafford, especially if you have no previous experience of the breed. Although these dogs are temperament tested and all of them deserve loving homes, they can sometimes be too challenging for the first-time owner and they will require 110 per cent commitment.

Many rescue dogs arrive with their own patterns of behaviour, which are already inherent, and some may never have been housetrained or they may require basic obedience training. If you feel able to cope with this, contact your local rescue centre and they will talk you through the whole process of adopting one of these dogs. Having said that, I have rescued Staffords and found the experience ultimately very rewarding.

Be aware that if you do decide to rescue one, it will involve a visit to your home to make sure that you – and your house – are suitable.

Puppy-proofing your home

Life for a Stafford puppy is one big adventure. These inquisitive babies will view almost anything they encounter as either a potential toy or food! Therefore, it is recommended that before you go ahead and welcome your new arrival into your home, you carry out the following checks inside and outside.

Outside

Make sure that your garden is secure. Stafford puppies have an amazing ability to squeeze through very small gaps in hedges and fencing, so mend any holes. It is also a good idea to check any gates or doors that lead into the garden, particularly at the bottom, where the gap from floor to gate should be no more than 5cm (2in).

Also bear in mind that the name Terrier comes from the word 'terrain', which means of the ground – these dogs enjoy digging, so protect any valuable plants. Check that you don't have any plants which are poisonous to dogs and be careful when using weed-killers and other chemicals. Cocoa mulch is also potentially dangerous if eaten.

This puppy has plenty of room to play, as well as fresh water and toys in a secure place.

Inside

You need to make the inside of your house puppy-proof, too. If you want to confine your puppy to certain rooms or the ground floor only, you could invest in a child-safety gate which can be placed in doorways or at the bottom of the stairs. Walk around your home, checking out the following:

Wires Puppies adore wires, so carefully check out any places where they may have access to loose wires, cables or electrical equipment and make sure that they are secure and out of harm's way.

Harmful substances Most of us keep bleach in the downstairs toilet or floor cleaner under the sink in the kitchen. Your new puppy will be quite happy to use these products as his playthings, so it is very important to make sure that any household cleaning materials and chemicals are well out of his reach or shut away securely in cupboards. Child safety locks fitted to cupboard doors are always a good option.

Chewing Tell the whole family to start keeping things tidy and not to leave anything that they value lying around, especially on the floor. You can try telling your new puppy that the designer trainer he has just eaten cost a lot of money or that the shredded paper at his feet was, in fact, a particularly important document, but he will not understand. Puppies love chewing and there is hardly anything they will not consider, so put things away or place them out of reach.

Puppies are happy to play in their crates for a while. It also gives them time to relax and sleep in their own den if they want.

Essential equipment

You will need to purchase some of the following items of equipment before you bring your new Stafford puppy home.

Crate and bedding

A crate is a metal or plastic 'home', and although some people think that crates are cruel prisons for dogs, this is far from the truth. When used correctly, they can help a puppy to settle into his new surroundings quickly. A crate will give him a sense of security, and it will enable you to housetrain him and make him feel secure. Most puppies soon learn that the crate is their own private place,

where they can sleep peacefully and escape from family life if they want to.

You can buy crates from dog shows, pet shops or via the internet. Remember that your puppy, who may fit in your hands now, will grow quickly, so buy a crate with plenty of room for your adult Stafford. Crates are great for travelling. They generally fit quite snugly in cars, and your dog will feel secure and safe.

Bedding comes in a variety of types, and specially made bedding can be obtained from the same sources as your crate. You may want to consider buying waterproof bedding for a new puppy as accidents will happen. However, a good blanket or two from your bed is just as good and this will allow the puppy to use his 'den-building' instincts, which survive in all dogs.

Playpens

Another great buy, which is particularly helpful when you are housetraining your puppy, is a wire playpen (a three-sided fireguard will also do the trick). It can easily be placed against a wall and will make a great (and cheap) alternative to an indoor crate. Do make sure that the sides of the playpen can be altered, to give your puppy enough room to sleep as well as a small play area.

His crate and playpen can be placed by your outside door and he should be encouraged to go outside in the garden to toilet from day one.

Remember, however, that your puppy should never be left in this confined environment for long periods, although it is perfect for night-times and those times during the day when you need to know where he is and to put him where he can see you. Puppies are like toddlers, so use that as your rule of thumb.

All puppies love to chew – even a cardboard tube or box can become a plaything.

Toys

All puppies love to chew and there is a good reason for this. Chewing is good not only for their mental wellbeing but can also physically aid the teething process. Remember that puppies are not dissimilar to babies, and the distraction of a few hard toys can avoid boredom.

Choose good-quality toys for young puppies, who will spend many happy hours playing.

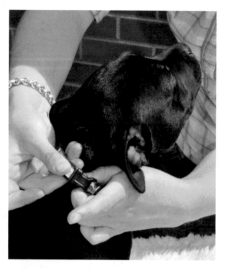

Get your new puppy acquainted with a soft 'puppy' collar. You should be able to insert three fingers if it is fit comfortably.

been. Your vet will be able to advise you on this (see page 102).

Secondly, a puppy's body in the first few months is growing fast and damage can occur to his immature bones if exercise is too rigorous. Having said this, however, it is a good idea to get your pup acquainted with wearing a collar as soon as possible. At first, buy a soft puppy collar and lead. There are many good collars designed for puppies. Make sure that the collar is soft – nylon is ideal – and a good fit; you should be able to comfortably fit your finger between the collar and the puppy's neck.

Don't worry if he fusses a little at first. He may try and scratch at the collar, or roll around as if trying to remove it. This is because it feels alien to him (imagine what it feels like when you wear a new hat or piece of jewellery for the first time). Leave him to it as this reaction won't last long, sometimes only minutes.

They also mean that your sofa and chair legs may remain intact. Staffords have a particularly strong chewing instinct, and therefore their toys should be chosen very carefully for maximum safety. Choose good-quality hard toys and try to avoid the cute furry ones, which will be demolished quickly and any fur or stuffing may be swallowed. Similarly, don't buy squeaky toys, which can soon be dismantled and contain small parts that are potentially very dangerous.

Collar and lead

For the first few weeks, you will be advised not to take your puppy out on a lead in public places. There are two reasons for this good advice: firstly, it is sensible to make sure that he has had all his vaccinations before venturing out into public places where other dogs have

Food and food bowls

Metal bowls are advisable, as plastic ones will be viewed as yet another thing to chew. Buy one for food and one for water. Some breeders recommend bowl stands (these are three- or four-legged raised containers) to prevent the puppy dipping his head to eat. Personally, I feel that normal feeding with the bowl on the floor is perfectly acceptable.

Ask the breeder what food the puppy has been weaned on. Most breeders will give you a diet sheet to take with you when you collect the puppy. Make sure you have the correct food ready for when the puppy arrives.

Wormers

Your breeder should have kept the puppy up-to-date with his worming, and your obligation will start the moment he arrives in your care. All dogs need to be wormed regularly in the first two years of their life. Your breeder or vet will be happy to advise you.

Flea prevention

As with worming, flea and tick control is an essential part of caring for your puppy. There are various excellent preventatives on the market and your vet can advise you and administer flea control for a nominal fee.

Bringing your puppy home

The day you collect your puppy will be very exciting. Make sure that at least two people (preferably adults) drive to pick him up. Puppies can get quite car sick at first and one of you will need to hold

Puppy training pads

These are like giant nappies that you place wherever you wish the puppy to toilet. Start by positioning one just outside his crate and then gradually move it closer to the door. He will soon associate the pad with doing his business and will 'follow' it to his ultimate destination… outside. Pads can also prevent too much mess on the floor.

him and make sure that he does not become distressed. Some people advise taking a cardboard box full of towels for the journey. However, although this may be a sensible precaution, I have brought a puppy home inside my coat, where the tiny creature was quite happy to sleep

Your puppy will soon associate his crate with security and will enjoy going in there.

Wearing a collar

Get your puppy used to wearing a collar for the first time. Give him a couple of days to settle in first, and then introduce him to it gently. Most puppies don't mind at all, but it will help with lead training if they grow accustomed to wearing a collar at the earliest possible age.

during the 200-mile journey.

You may want to ask the breeder for a scrap of bedding which has the scent of the puppy's mother on it, as it can be quite soothing for him if he can still smell something familiar amongst his new surroundings.

If your journey will be lengthy, remember to take a bottle of water and a small bowl with you in the car. If a toilet break becomes necessary, you can pull up somewhere well away from the traffic and stay close to your puppy until he has relieved himself.

Settling in at home

When you arrive home, introduce your puppy to your garden straight away. This will tell him that this is where he can relieve himself. Next stop should be his bed, which may be a crate, or a dog bed lined with old towels or blankets. Avoid fluffy bedding as your puppy will probably end up chewing most of it. Some people use sturdy cardboard boxes as first beds. These are OK, but you may find a huge pile of shredded cardboard and no bed the next morning.

Leave him to settle quietly and allow him to have a potter round and explore the house. Remember that this can be

Most puppies soon get used to wearing a collar and lead. Put them on your dog and let him trail them round the garden.

quite an overwhelming experience, and even though Staffords are generally very adaptable, your puppy has just left his mother and litter mates and has entered a whole new world, all in one day. If you have children, don't let them overwhelm him. Explain to them that he needs peace and quiet while he settles in and when he feels more confident he will probably want to play. Young dogs need plenty of sleep and, much like their human counterparts, will probably eat, sleep and toilet for the first few weeks of their life.

House-training

If done properly, house-training can be easy and stress-free for both you and your puppy. No puppy can avoid having the odd accident. He will have lived in a confined space for the first eight weeks of his life and will probably have relieved himself on newspaper. So don't expect him to know automatically what to do straight away. You need to be patient.

In the very early stages, make sure that he is able to reach some newspaper (or a training pad) the minute he leaves his bed. He will be used to doing this,

Always reward your puppy with praise words when he toilets outside in the garden.

and any immediate change from his usual routine may cause him undue stress.

It is ideal if his crate can be positioned as near to the outside door (the one he will go out of to relieve himself) as possible. This newspaper training will teach him not only to go in the same place all the time but will also help him to associate the back door with his toilet.

During the first week, try and observe the times that he needs to toilet and start pre-empting him. Most puppies relieve themselves after a meal and on waking, so start off by taking him outside first

Playtime

A Stafford puppy is happiest when he is playing. Until he has been fully vaccinated and is happy to walk on a lead, it is best to restrict his exercise to playtime with you in the garden and around the home.

Staffords love to tug things, so gentle tugs-of-war with a dog rope (available wherever dog toys can be obtained) are a good idea. Be careful with your puppy's teeth though, and don't be too boisterous at this stage. Let him chase toys that you throw for him and encourage him to run around the garden with you as well. If he is good, and particularly if he is gentle, reward his behaviour with a small dog treat and plenty of praise. Remember that at this age a puppy will tire very easily, so don't expect too much from him: 10–15 minutes at a time are sufficient.

thing in the morning. Don't worry if he has already done something on his newspaper. Stand with him and let him toilet; maybe say a special word to get him used to the routine, such as 'Be quick'. If he performs, make a fuss of him and praise him enthusiastically before taking him back inside. He will learn that toileting outside in a particular spot is rewarding and will want to please you.

After a couple of weeks, he may go to the door himself and ask to be put out. Let him out and never stop using praise as this will reinforce that what he is doing is right. At this point, start telling him it is wrong to toilet inside. However, you must remain patient and not shout at your puppy. Make sure the door is open for him whenever possible. If you see him squatting down in readiness inside the house, use a single word command, such as 'No' or 'Outside', then pick him up and carry him outside. Praise him lavishly when he does his job.

This simple method will eventually produce the right result, but remember that accidents will happen occasionally, that a mixture of praise and commands will work, and that shouting will get you nowhere at all but will only frighten and confuse him. Be consistent and prepared to take your puppy outside 20 times a day if necessary, and you will soon have a dog who tells you when he needs the toilet – not the other way around.

It is best at this stage to stay outside with your puppy to make sure that he is doing his business, not just sneaking out of sight and pretending he has if the weather does not quite suit him.

Take advice from your breeder on feeding your Stafford puppy in the first few weeks.

Feeding

Your breeder will provide you with a diet sheet, so try and follow this as closely as possible as it will mirror the puppy's early regime and avoid possible stomach upsets caused by a sudden change in his diet. If you wish to change your young Stafford's diet for some reason, do so gradually over a couple of weeks, slowly introducing more of the new food and less of the old. It is unwise at this age to change his diet radically.

Until your puppy is about 20 weeks old, I would recommend four small meals a day: breakfast, mid-morning, mid-afternoon and a final one at around 7pm. A good handful of food is a rough guide for each meal. Meals that are too large can cause your puppy to become overweight and may stretch his stomach.

Ideal meals at this stage are scrambled eggs with a little grated cheese, small bite mixers and a small amount of gravy or fish (fresh or canned in oil or brine, not tomato-based sauces).

Some breeders recommend feeding at different times to give the dog a good feeding 'instinct', whereas others advise sticking to a strict routine. I have known dogs thrive on both plans and Staffords are rarely fussy eaters, so do what works best for you and your dog.

Which foods?
For the first 18 months, feed your dog a good-quality food designed specifically for his age. Most food manufacturers have complete foods designed for puppies, juniors and adult dogs. If you want to feed dry food, make sure that plenty of fresh water is available. If you prefer to feed fresh food, e.g. tripe or minced meat, you can add a little dry food, too. Cooked vegetables can also be added to meals.

There are two types of commercially available dog food: complete dried and canned. Both have a place in a dog's diet and both will undoubtedly be used by you at some point. Complete food is, as its name suggests, a dried food that contains all the nutrients your dog needs in one meal. It can be fed dry or with water or gravy added for moisture. If dry, ensure that plenty of fresh water is available.

Canned, or pouch, food is usually a meat-based food, often containing lamb, chicken or beef, along with vegetables and rice and a rich gravy. Ideal for a quick meal, served with a dry mixer, it is available from most supermarkets.

If you suspect your puppy is off his food, or has a slight tummy upset, cooked long-grain rice and a small amount of chicken can be fed in place of richer food.

Lastly, it may sound obvious, but make sure that a bowl of fresh water is available at all times for your puppy, and remember to refill it regularly.

Grooming
It is a good idea to get your puppy accustomed to being groomed from the earliest possible age, so he comes to accept being handled and enjoys this special time with you. Staffords do not require much grooming – just a quick session with a rubber grooming tool to keep their coat healthy and shiny. At the same time, check your puppy's ears and eyes, and inspect his claws – the nails may need clipping.

Grooming is a great way to get your Stafford puppy accustomed to being handled.

Chapter 3

Socialization and training

When you take the decision to own a Stafford, you must realize that you will have to dedicate considerable time and patience to his socialization and training. This dog's bold temperament can lead some people to generalize that he is stubborn and difficult to train, but, in fact, nothing could be further from the truth. This breed excels in both obedience and agility, two of the most disciplined canine activities. Staffords are incredibly intelligent and eager to learn from a very young age, which, in turn, makes them relatively easy to train.

What now?

By the time your puppy is 12 weeks old, he should have had all the necessary vaccinations from your vet and will be ready to be introduced to the world. Although his early socialization should have been initiated by his breeder, it is now your job to carry on this training.

He will already be used to the feel of a collar around his neck, and should be able to wear it most of the time without even noticing it. You should also be able to handle him a little by the collar without him looking too bemused. If you have children, he has probably already been 'led' somewhere by the collar.

He should also have been introduced to plenty of different people and dogs, either yours or ones belonging to friends and neighbours. These experiences will have taught him some valuable lessons and created a world where new things and experiences will be enjoyable for him. Be aware that puppies around two to

Introducing other dogs at an early age will make for a well-socialized Stafford.

Opposite: Staffords are very intelligent and relatively easy to train. Remember this cute bundle will grow into a strong, muscular adult.

three months of age may go through a period where they appear nervous about new experiences. This is nothing for you to worry about, and it is your job to reassure your puppy. Be careful not to praise nervousness or 'aggression' towards whatever has bothered him, as this will enforce the idea that he is behaving correctly. Simply remove him from the problem, and praise him only when his reaction becomes positive, which will happen eventually.

Children

The Stafford is often affectionately called the 'Nanny Dog'. This name obviously refers to his immense love of children, and there truly is no dog who is more fond of youngsters and protective of them. Children and puppies are often

a match made in heaven, and his stoic nature and resistance to pain mean that there is not much he will not tolerate when it comes to his young family. However, always remember that children should never be left unsupervised with any dog, and most incidences of dogs snapping at them (and this applies to all breeds) are a direct result of a child hurting or startling the dog when they are unsupervised.

Socializing your puppy around children can be one of the best parts of his training; the pleasure of seeing the interaction between them is wonderful. Don't forget that his introduction to

The Stafford is a wonderful companion to children – he is not known as the Nanny Dog for nothing! Like with other breeds, always supervise children with the dog.

children should be carried out gently and that they should be taught to treat their new dog with love and respect in order to develop a good relationship with him. A child's natural excitement and enthusiasm around the puppy must be monitored. Equally, children must not be afraid to carefully handle the puppy under adult supervision. This is good training for both of them.

Out and about

As soon as your Stafford puppy has been vaccinated and knows his name, it's time to begin introducing him to the world outside his front door. From moving in with you, he will have been called constantly by his name. You will have called him to you, told him that his food is ready and that it's time for his toilet.

Introduce your Stafford to as many different breeds of dog and as many different situations as you can while he is young.

This gentle calling of his name over the last few weeks will have already started the ball rolling: as you can see, he now knows his name.

People like to introduce their Stafford to new experiences as soon as possible, and this is recommended to socialize him early. I have even sat with a six-week-old puppy inside my coat at a bus stop, in the rain, simply to get him used to traffic. The main thing is that you want your Stafford to be comfortable in many different situations, and the only way to guarantee this is to introduce him to as many things and experiences as you can, as soon as you can. Traffic, trains,

bicycles, wind, rain, children, adults, balls, other dogs… the list is endless.

At this critical point in your puppy's development, you must make sure that bad experiences are avoided at all costs, as these can have a lasting effect on him. A child who pulls his tail too hard or a bad encounter with another dog can cause negative feelings in your puppy, which may take time to heal. Be careful, and never let him off the lead at this stage to play with other dogs. Always supervise any meetings with children, particularly ones who are strangers. This may sound worrying but it is not; you are merely making sure that the experiences he has are fun – you are not watching him so much as being circumspect with the people he meets.

Remember that everything is new to your puppy and you must handle each situation individually. This pup is enthusiastically following his mother with the food bowl.

Staffords are both intelligent and inquisitive. Daft as it may sound, some dogs can take a dislike to certain things, such as spectacles, beards, uniforms or ties. Therefore, let your puppy meet the postman and your local community officer and get him used to as many different things as possible now, so, he won't get phased by them as he matures.

You will require plenty of patience in these 'teen' weeks. Puppies are like blank pages at this age, and anything that you do will imprint itself on your dog's eager-to-please mind. It is thought that the complete training of your dog can continue until he is about two years of age, so starting early simply gives you – and him – a good head start.

Training classes
It is a really good idea at this stage to find a local dog training or ringcraft club. These are usually held in the evenings by canine societies and breed clubs, and they are an ideal way not only to socialize your Stafford but also to give you the chance to learn from people who really know what they are talking about. Ideally, try and find a Staffordshire Bull Terrier Club in your area so that you and your puppy can meet other Staffords face to face. You can find your nearest club by checking with the Kennel Club (see page 126).

Whilst these classes are a great idea for general socialization, they may not focus too much on the basic commands, such as 'Sit', 'Stay' and 'Down'. However, these basics are well within your reach as his principal trainer, and we will cover them later on in this chapter in more detail (see page 51).

Ringcraft classes are one of the best ways to introduce your Stafford to other well-socialized dogs, meet like-minded people and get him accustomed to being handled, petted and generally messed around with. As well as this, there will be breed people there who will help you with basic commands, such as 'Stand' and 'Walk', and will be happy to dispense with as much free advice as you want.

Don't be embarrassed if your puppy plays up and refuses to do anything you ask the first time you attend. This is all

Other dogs
Staffords can sometimes be capable of dog-to-dog aggression (see page 82). It is part of their heritage and, whilst most are bred now for sound temperaments, the fact remains that other dogs (and, in particular, other Staffords) can arouse their historic 'gameness'. It is therefore vital that your puppy's early experiences with other dogs are always good ones, and he must learn from you that any feelings of aggression towards them will not be tolerated. It is never acceptable for a Stafford to be allowed free rein to display this type of aggression.

Generally, a Stafford who has not received an adequate amount of exposure to other dogs (especially other Staffords) may cause problems as he gets older, larger and stronger. There can only ever be one master/pack leader in the human/dog relationship and that is you. These early days are a vital time when you should be teaching your Stafford puppy this lesson.

new to him (as well as to you). If he sits down when he is asked to 'Walk', and walks when you ask him to 'Stand', don't worry. We all have to start somewhere and there will be plenty of people there who have seen it all before and will be able to help and advise you. Never be afraid to admit your ignorance and ask them for advice.

Don't believe anyone who tells you that a puppy of three or four months is still too young to attend classes or be trained by you. As soon as your puppy's vaccination course is complete and you get the all-clear from your vet, you can start. Effective communication between you and your dog from the moment he arrives will ensure success.

A positive attitude

Nowadays dog owners are encouraged to practise what is known as positive training. This is relatively self-explanatory: in a nutshell, it means that dogs are trained using a combination of rewards (in the form of food treats) and praise. There is no need to ever use force or harsh words when you are training your Stafford – the use of a firm 'No' should be all that is required to tell your dog that he is doing something wrong. Another good way to 'punish' any unwanted behaviour in your Stafford is simply to withhold treats. If you ask for a certain action to be obeyed and then he ignores you, do not follow this with a treat, even if you have one in your hand ready to give to him.

All dogs are truly creatures of habit and the simple basic rules of rewarding good behaviour and not rewarding bad behaviour will very quickly be absorbed by your dog's brain.

Staffords love to dig. A firm 'No' if you catch him red-handed should do the trick!

Successful training

The two essential words to remember when you're training your Stafford are discipline and continuity. Any training programme will succeed if you remain disciplined in your approach and use repetition throughout. Your dog will soon learn to associate certain words with specific actions, followed by praise and a reward. This, essentially, is the basis of successful training.

Always remember that your Stafford is an intelligent dog and he will be as easy to train as any other breed if you are firm and fair. All dogs have inborn instincts – just like humans – although they obviously lack the rational thought processes that govern our own behaviour, and rely almost wholly on their instincts. It would be foolish to compare dogs' minds with those of their owners, but dogs do have quite long memories as well as a sense of right and wrong, albeit to a very limited degree. Therefore it is always worth remembering that no matter how well trained your Stafford is, his instincts can rise to the fore in the blink of an eye, particularly if he feels threatened. Never become complacent and think that your dog is bombproof (no dog is), even though with good training there is every chance that he will be well behaved in all situations.

Before we move on to the basic commands, there is just one more point worth noting. Occasionally, un-neutered males can be slightly more dominant than either bitches or neutered males. This not written in stone, but bear in mind that they can be slightly less

Patience and perseverance are the two key words during training. Always be sure to reward your puppy's good behaviour.

responsive in the early stages of training. If this is the case, persevere – you will get there in the end.

Basic obedience

To have a well-trained Stafford is vital. In fact, no breed of dog is ever totally reliable unless the basics of obedience have been taught. The guidance in the following pages will help you to gain control over your Stafford in a gentle but firm manner and, along the way, will give you a dog who will obey your commands quickly and happily.

Get your dog's attention

The most important thing you can have when you begin training your Stafford is his full attention. Ask any primary school teacher whether they can teach anything to young children without first gaining their full attention and their answer will be 'No'. Similarly, it is almost impossible to teach a dog anything if he is bored and not focused.

A good time to train your puppy is when he is alert. So don't try training him just after feeding or exercise: a puppy who is tired or full up will not make for a good pupil. Your Stafford's attention span at this young age will be fairly short, although the fact that you will be using treats to reward him will mean that it may last slightly longer than normal. However, try not to spend more than 15 minutes maximum per session as this can quickly lead to boredom. The more fun your puppy is having, the more quickly he will learn. Several short training sessions spread out throughout the day and repeated regularly will be more effective than just one long session.

Using treats

I strongly recommend using treats as a form of praise when beginning your basic training. This will ensure that you have your dog's attention at all times (no Stafford can resist a treat) and will be your way of rewarding him when he gets something right. Food will not be used once his training is complete. The tidbits used initially are there in order to implement your commands and to establish good behaviour.

There are lots of good treats available, but don't use big ones – you only need very small pieces of a dog stick (flat meat-flavoured treats) or perhaps some canine chocolate drops. Specially formulated chocolate drops for dogs are good, but never offer human chocolate, as this can actually be harmful to dogs, even in relatively small quantities.

Choosing commands

You will be using various commands for your basic training, such as 'Sit', 'Stay', 'Walk' and 'Down'. It is important to remember that your young Stafford does not understand English, and these words will mean nothing to him, although he will eventually learn to differentiate between a small number of key words. The important thing is to get your dog accustomed to the different tones of voice you use for different actions.

Decide on the praise words you will use, which are generally 'Good boy', 'Good girl' or 'Well done', and always use the same words. Your puppy will then associate them with an action he has performed well. Tell your family to use the same words and not variants, which will only serve to confuse the dog.

Who does the training?

Ideally, training your Stafford should be a family affair. This does not mean that you all stand on the sidelines shouting commands, which will get you nowhere. What I advise is that your dog should be aware that all the humans in his home are to be obeyed. It's little use having him respond to only one member of the family and ignore everybody else. It is advisable that adults begin the initial training, but let your children sit quietly and watch. In this way, you will all be using the same commands and the same tone of voice, which will make the dog's training far easier.

Don't ever allow young children to take your Stafford out on a lead alone. Do not run the risk of him seeing a cat or being startled by something whilst out walking, as his strength could easily pull a child over and cause injury.

Do include young children in walks and lead training; simply let them walk alongside the dog, perhaps with their hand placed gently on his collar while you hold the lead. However, this should not be done in the early stages of lead training, as it will only confuse the dog, who may want to play rather than concentrate on the task in hand.

Be sure to praise your puppy and make a fuss of him every time he does something you have asked him to do. This will help to reinforce the good behaviour.

Lead training

There are two stages of training a puppy: on the lead and off the lead. All your dog's initial training should be done on the lead where possible. At the moment, your young Stafford is still a bit of an unknown quantity; in other words, he has not learned yet how to behave in certain situations. If he decides to run away whilst you are trying to get him to sit down, the training will take much longer and may not work at all.

Walking on the lead

One of the first things you need to do is to make sure that your Stafford knows how to behave on the end of his lead. A good place to start lead training is in the garden (if there are no distractions) or indoors.

Use a treat or favourite toy to keep your puppy focused and reward him. Keep this in your hand at all times, so that he has something to concentrate on.

Lead problems

There are three main reactions to walking on the lead (see opposite) that will need working on. Don't despair if your dog has problems initially – with time, patience and the correct approach, they can be remedied.

1 Start with your puppy on the lead on your left-hand side, holding the lead in your left hand. Make sure you have a treat concealed in your right hand.

2 Move off with your left foot first and give the command 'Walk'. Your dog will begin to associate your tone of voice and the word with the desired action.

3 If your dog moves ahead of you, reach down the lead and gently pull him back from about halfway down the lead. This is called short leash walking, and he will soon realize that he has to stay level with you (not in front of you).

4 Use praise as soon as he becomes level with you again. If he refuses to move, show him the treat and use the command again until he does. When he walks correctly beside you on the lead without pulling, reward him with the treat.

Dragging or collapsing

This behaviour occurs when the puppy refuses to walk on the lead. He may lie down and refuse to move or he may adopt a submissive position, with his head down, almost as if he is trying to let the collar slip over his head. To prevent this happening, you must use constant praise and reassurance to encourage him to walk, as his reaction may suggest a lack of confidence. Call his name and use either a treat or his favourite toy to coax him forward. Under no circumstances, try to drag him forward – this will not work.

Training tips

- Use plenty of praise throughout and don't use the lead roughly
- Never yank your dog on the lead, as this will not teach him anything. As with all training, you need bags of patience and perseverance
- Once the ability to walk by your side has been established, you will find that your Stafford will be able to have a longer lead and still remain by your side.

Pulling

We have all laughed at the poor owner being taken for a walk by his dog, but, in reality, this behaviour is undesirable and can, in the worst cases, indicate dominant canine behaviour. Indeed, the strength of a fully-grown Stafford can easily pull a person over, so nip this behaviour in the bud now while your dog is still young. If your Stafford forges ahead of you on the lead, all you have to do is stop walking. Get him to come back to you and stand by your side, then set off again. Repeat this as often as necessary with plenty of praise when your dog walks alongside you and there is no tension on the lead.

Never engage in a war of strength with your Stafford by pulling back; this will only add to the problem, not stop it. Your dog will soon learn that if he wants to walk, he cannot pull or you will just stop and he will get nowhere.

Jumping up

This is a very common problem: your puppy will jump and bound around, literally climbing up the lead. This can be due to excitement, but it must not be encouraged. Use the command 'No' and make your puppy sit before setting off again. Repeat every time until he learns that he will not go for his walks until he stops jumping up.

Being pulled along by a Stafford may amuse onlookers, but it is important to teach your puppy that this is not acceptable. If he starts to pull, stop walking immediately.

> ## Training tip
> You may want to start asking your dog to sit before you feed him or whilst you attach his lead before going out for a walk. Indeed, you can ask him to do this before doing anything pleasurable, as this will quickly reinforce the command in his mind, so he obeys immediately.

'Sit'

This is one of the most basic and useful commands you can teach your dog. Again, make sure that your puppy is relaxed before you begin. After a couple of weeks' training, he should respond to the verbal command without the use of a treat. The sit is a good command to have under your belt, and is great to use when you are waiting to cross roads or when travelling on public transport.

Note: If your dog remains standing, use the command 'Sit' again and, keeping the treat out of reach and above him, gently push down on his rear. Praise and reward him when he performs the required action.

1 Holding a treat in your right hand, call your puppy to a position where he is standing directly in front of you. Use a lead initially when teaching this command, especially if he does not stand by you or wanders off.

2 When he is in place, gradually raise the hand holding the treat to a position just above his head. This will force his head to come up and he may naturally assume the sitting position.

3 As soon as you see his back legs start to bend and his bottom goes down, use the command 'Sit'. When he sits down, reward him immediately with the treat and use lots of praise.

'Down'

Before you start teaching this command, it is important to remember that in your dog's mind lying down is a submissive position.

As such, it is vital that training him to lie down is never done forcefully, as this will only instill a feeling of fear and he may try to nip anyone who tries too hard to get him to lie down. Failing that, he may just run away. You must get him to lie down without him feeling threatened by assuming this position.

Note: If this does not work, you may have to resort to pressing down very gently on your dog's back, just behind his neck and the top of his shoulders as you say 'Down'. Remember that this is a gentle hint, and you must never press hard or use sudden movements.

Training tip

As with all other commands, the more repetitive the training the sooner you will succeed. Ask your dog to lie down whilst out walking or in the house in the evening – in fact, anywhere. As previously stated, the food incentive can be dropped as soon as the command alone is fully understood.

1 Start with your dog on a lead, standing to the side of you but facing the same way. Make sure that you have a treat in your free hand.

2 Bend down and, with the food firmly in your hand at floor level, slide it along the ground slowly in front of your dog to encourage him to follow it.

3 As he starts to go down to get the food, give him the command 'Down'. Keep him in this position for about 15–30 seconds, praising him lavishly and reassuring him that he has done well. Give him the treat when you are satisfied that his 'lie down' has been successful.

'Stay'

This is a useful command, which can be practised at different times of the day, especially while you are preparing your dog's food, which will ultimately become his reward for the stay. This can often be easier than using a treat for teaching this particular command. Staffords love their food and the lure of a treat can sometimes overpower their owner's command to stay. However, try it with the treat as well, and see how it goes.

Note that the stay is easier to teach when your dog has successfully mastered the basic commands for sit (see page 51) and down (see page 52) training.

Note: If your dog's rear comes up, don't give the treat, but go back to his side and try again. Remember that the treat should only be given if he stays still.

Taking it further

After 7–10 days, you can start to move a little further away. Do exactly the same

1 Start teaching the stay with your dog on the lead in front of you. Hold the lead in one hand and a tasty treat in the other hand.

2 Tell your dog to 'Sit' and make sure that the hand with the treat in it is near his nose, so he can smell it. You need him to be aware that it is there.

as before, but rather than stand right in front of him, hold the treat up and move a little bit further away.

Use the command 'Stay' and let your Stafford see the food you are holding in your raised hand. You can then start to move progressively further and further away and leave him for longer periods. Always praise and reward him when he obeys. To release him from the stay, you need to teach him to come when called (see page 56).

Training off the lead

By now you should feel comfortable that your Stafford will accept the commands we have discussed. Don't worry if you have the odd hiccup, but make sure you feel confident enough with his 'on the lead' training before you start working on any 'off the lead' commands. It is still best to practise these at home or in the garden rather than in a public place where he may get distracted by other dogs and people.

3 Once he has obeyed and is in the sitting position, give the command 'Stay', while stepping back a little and away from him.

4 You should still be very close to your dog and allow him to nuzzle the food. If he does not move, give him the treat and praise him immediately.

'Come'

You will already have started this training the minute your new puppy arrived in your home. Every time you called his name, perhaps bending down and patting your knees or clicking your fingers, you were teaching him his first command. To teach the word 'Come' you can adopt much the same method.

Training tip

This basic command is a great way to start teaching your Stafford. More essentially, it will teach him that responding to your voice commands will end in praise and a treat – two of his favourite things. At this stage, it is not a good idea to practise the 'Come' command outdoors in a public space. This can be done only when you are confident in your dog's reactions to your commands.

I Ask someone to hold your puppy and ensure that he is relaxed and you have his attention. He should be aware that you are holding a treat in your hand.

2 Ask the person to release him and then call his name. As soon as your puppy starts to walk towards you, say the command 'Come' clearly.

3 As he gets nearer to you, bend down towards him and welcome him, repeating the command 'Come'. Get right down to his level, give him the treat and then use your praise word.

Note: If you are confident that your dog is beginning to understand, train him to come to you from further away by extending the distance between you by a stride every couple of days.

'Sit', 'Stay' and 'Down'

All these commands can – and should eventually – be obeyed off the lead. Follow the steps you have learnt for each command but without a lead. This should be relatively easy if the on-the-lead training has been followed. Continue to use tasty treats as a reward and decrease them as the commands are more fully understood by your dog.

Never try any off-lead training in open or public places at this stage. There may be moments when commands are not obeyed; additionally, there will be too many distractions for you to have your Stafford's full attention.

Training problems

Before concluding this training section, I must cover a common problem you may encounter. Whilst this is certainly not behavioural, you will reap the benefits of dealing with it now rather than struggling later on. Remember that Staffords are extremely intelligent dogs but they can be willful and headstrong. The following advice may require you to exercise a more hands-on approach, albeit a gentle one.

Refusal of commands

A Stafford who refuses to obey the basic commands 'Sit' and 'Down' may simply be tired or bored. He may also find that the offer of an edible treat is insufficient to make him do the required action, perhaps because he has just eaten a meal and is full. If this is the case, then you could try using a squeaky toy instead or practise your training at some other time when he is more receptive and you have his full attention.

Refusal to sit

If you find that saying the command 'Sit' while raising the hand that is holding the treat is not working, try holding your dog's collar in one hand and pushing down very gently on his hindquarters with the other. Use the command 'Sit' as you do this. Praise your dog lavishly and make a fuss of him as soon as he sits down.

Refusal to lie down

Similarly, a refusal by your Stafford to lie down on the 'Down' command will require you to kneel by your puppy. From a sitting position, gently lift up his front legs (imagine that you are putting him into a begging position) and then lay his front legs out straight on the floor, giving the command 'Down' as you do so.

Reward him well with plenty of praise and a tasty treat. As already mentioned, some dogs can find this position submissive, so always make sure that you are down at your Stafford's level to do this; it will mean that he does not feel threatened by you.

The last word

Remember that training is supposed to be fun for you and your dog, so have fun together and enjoy these training sessions. Treat them as a way of getting to know each other better and bonding rather than as a disagreeable chore. Always stay cheerful and firm throughout and never get irritable or lose your temper when your dog does not perform the desired behaviour. If the session is not progressing well, just stop and try some other time when he is in the mood.

Opposite: Training is supposed to be fun for both you and your dog and it will help you to form an unbreakable bond.

Chapter 4

Your adult dog

By the time he is two years old, your Stafford should be fully mature, and although dogs reach this stage at different times, this is a relatively good rule of thumb. By now he should be a fully-fledged member of your family and will be used to a regular daily routine, including feeding, exercising, playing games, grooming and travelling in the car or on the bus with you.

The advice in the following pages will give you a rough guide to your dog's day-to-day care. Remember that nothing is set in stone, and you will eventually find your own routine that best suits both you and your dog.

Feeding

Moving from puppy to adult feeding should be done at around 18 months. Up until this age, your dog will have been growing steadily and 'filling out' his frame but now he will need an adult maintenance diet.

A natural diet

A dog's teeth and digestive system are designed to tear meat and to digest it accordingly. In the wild, dogs live on a diet of raw meat, skin, bone and fur.

Opposite: Adult Staffords thrive on routine, so try not to make any sudden changes to your dog's daily routine.

What not to do

- No matter how tempting it is, and no matter how big, brown and soulful are the eyes looking up at you, never feed your dog from the table whilst you eat. In fact, make sure your Stafford knows that begging at the dinner table is not allowed. The food we eat can often contain amounts of fat, salt and seasoning that are not good for a dog.
- Meals should be of a consistency where your dog has to chew the food well. Mature dogs should not be fed meals that resemble soup with bits of food floating around in them.
- Dogs don't need regular changes once you have found a food that suits them. Unlike humans, a Stafford will happily eat the same meal every day.

Dogs are omnivores and also benefit from vegetables in their diet. They have very strong gastric juices, which break down food in the stomach, and they are capable of eating – and digesting – relatively substantial meals all in one go. I have always fed my adult dogs just one good meal a day, usually in the early evening.

Bearing all this in mind, it is essential to feed your dog meals consisting of meat and roughage, which essentially replaces the hair, skin and bone to aid good digestion. I have opted for a more natural home-cooked diet for my dogs and have always fed them beef mince, tripe, lamb mince, ox heart and liver. I feed these with a good-quality 'mixer', which is a savoury biscuit and full of fibre. You can buy all the above from good pet shops or superstores, or from your local butcher. All the meat can be dry-fried before being added to the biscuit meal, although I occasionally give the beef mince raw, and my Staffords love it. Tuna and salmon are also great, but you may have to save up for those. Oily fish is great for your dog's teeth, bones and coat. I sometimes add a little olive oil to their food, which also gives their coat a wonderful healthy sheen.

It is OK to add leftovers to your Stafford's food. Cooked vegetables from your Sunday lunch, cooked meats and gravy are all great and your dog will really enjoy them. However, don't add anything salty or over-seasoned.

It is important to discover a feeding regime that suits both you and your dog.

Dried and canned food

If all this sounds rather time consuming – and, let's face it, all of us with work commitments may not have the time to indulge our dogs in gourmet offerings – there are plenty of complete dried foods and canned meat products, which are more convenient alternatives. You can experiment with different brands to find the one that suits your Stafford.

How many meals?

Nowadays there is a train of thought that suggests your dog should be fed two or three small meals a day rather than one larger one. The reasoning behind this is that dogs who are fed smaller, more frequent meals are more laid back and less likely to beg. I personally have never found this to be the case and feed mine once a day. Find out what suits you and your dog and try to stick to it.

How much food?

A rough guide as to what amount to feed your adult Stafford daily is 500g (1lb 2oz) of dried food (or equivalent) – 100g (3½oz) is about a teacupful. Keep an eye on how your Stafford seems to be doing on this amount, and use your eyes and hands to check for weight gain or loss.

Staffords who are exercised for two or more hours a day will naturally need more food than those dogs who only do half an hour's walking.

Be careful if you think that your dog is gaining weight – a fat Stafford is rarely happy. A good way to tell is to stand behind him and to look down at him. A Stafford's back end is often referred to

Does his diet suit him?

A good diet should always mean a happy and healthy dog. Outward signs to look for are a shiny coat, wet nose and clear, sparkling eyes. There should be no signs of flaking skin (which looks like dandruff), which can indicate that a change in diet is needed. Signs that may indicate that your dog's diet needs some fine-tuning can be one or more of the following:

• Excessive wind
• Large, very frequent or runny faeces
• Allergic reactions, e.g. to grass or fleas
• Eating plants or grass
• Eating his own faeces
• Unusual itching, scratching or biting where other factors have been ruled out by your vet.

Note: If you do notice any of these warning signs, try changing your dog's food. It may take a little time until you find the right one, but the symptoms should slowly disappear with the right food.

as being like a 'tadpole' – broad at the shoulders, tapering to a slightly thinner back end. If you can see his stomach sticking out on both sides, then you may need to cut back on your dog's food and increase his exercise.

As your dog approaches his senior years (from about seven years onwards), he may need slightly less food per meal; there are also some great 'senior' feeds available, which take this into account.

And if you are still confused about whether you are feeding your dog the right foods in the correct amounts, do remember that your breeder or vet will be happy to give you advice if you feel worried about his diet.

Grooming your dog

Staffords are relatively low-maintenance dogs when it comes to coat care. A good traditional bristle brush or a hand brush (which you put on your hand rather like a glove) is ideal for giving your dog a quick grooming session. Some people advocate brushing your Stafford every day, but I only tend to brush mine once or twice a week, unless I am exhibiting them at a dog show.

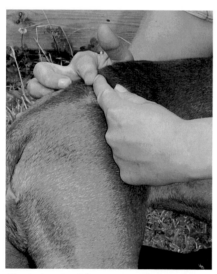

Check your Stafford's coat regularly for any unusual lumps and bumps as well as signs of fleas or mite infestation.

Brush your dog where it will be easy to clear his hair up. Although Staffords don't moult badly, a good brush will certainly dislodge enough hairs to make a mess of your carpet. Brush the coat firmly all over to remove any dead hair and stimulate the natural oils that give the coat its wonderful shine.

A good tip is to have a piece of cloth handy, such as some chamois, satin or even velvet. Rubbing your dog's coat with this will give it a beautiful gleam and is something that show dogs often get a quick rub down with before going into the show ring to be judged.

Check-ups

Grooming sessions with your Stafford are also an ideal time to check him over healthwise. The following checks can all be carried out easily, probably without him even noticing.

• Check his ears and eyes; they should be clean with no discharge
• As you run your hands over him, check for any lumps or bumps
• Although fleas are invisible to the naked eye, look for signs of coat disturbance or baldness, which may suggest your dog has been scratching
• Staffords can also be susceptible to grass allergies, which manifest themselves as sore and itchy looking stomachs. Contact your vet if you suspect that this is the case.

Finally, use these sessions as a great opportunity to strengthen your bond with your Stafford. However, be aware that they should not be treated as playtimes, more as relaxation.

Grooming routine

Grooming your Stafford regularly gives you both a chance to spend time together and relax. Your dog should enjoy this quality time with you. It is also an opportunity to check him over physically.

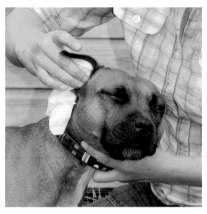

1 Use a good rubber handbrush or dog brush to take out any loose hairs and to stimulate the natural coat oils.

2 You can gently clean the inside of your dog's ears with a damp sponge, some cotton wool or a clean cloth.

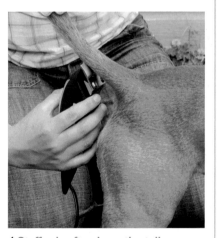

3 Special combs (which can be obtained from pet shops) can take out any dead hair in the coat, but use them gently.

4 Staffords often have the tail on their hair 'razored' to give a slick finish. Ask your breeder for advice before attempting this.

Nail care

Plenty of roadwork in his exercise should mean that your Stafford's nails are kept well worn down. Nail care should be something to which he is accustomed, as long nails are unattractive and they can tear and bleed. If you can hear your dog's nails 'clicking' on the floor as he walks, then it is probably time for a trim. Never use ordinary scissors to cut his nails; you can buy specially designed clippers from pet stores.

If you are planning to cut your dog's nails yourself, you must be very careful. The toenail contains a blood vessel, which is known as the 'quick'. If this vessel is accidentally cut, it can bleed quite profusely and, as it contains nerves, can also be very painful for your dog. If a nail does start to bleed, you can apply pressure with a cotton wool ball or a tissue. Reassuring your Stafford all the time will avoid him panicking. Staffords have black nails, so it is very difficult to ascertain where the quick is. Why not ask your breeder or vet to show you how to trim the nails before you attempt it yourself at home?

Take your dog's paw in one hand and clip about 3mm (^{1}/8in) off any nails that look too long. It is best to be decisive once you start, as dogs rarely 'enjoy' having their nails clipped, so make the experience as short lived as you can. If you still feel worried about cutting your dog's nails, you can always opt out and ask your vet to do it for you.

If you feel worried about clipping your Stafford's nails, ask your vet to do it for you.

Dental care

It may surprise you that you can buy meat-flavoured toothpaste for dogs as well as their own toothbrush. Joking apart, it is wise to keep your Stafford's teeth clean. Although our dogs do not eat the kinds of food that are usually associated with tooth decay, they do suffer from the same sort of problems as humans, including the build up of tartar and bad breath.

Remember that a dog having his teeth brushed is a fairly bizarre experience, but get your Stafford used to it from an early age and he will benefit from a clean and healthy mouth with a reduced risk of tooth decay and missing teeth as he gets older. Brush his teeth a couple of times a week – more often if you feed him moist, canned dog food.

You can ask your butcher for a good knucklebone as these are wonderful for keeping teeth clean. The gnawing action will remove stains and tartar and your Stafford will appreciate your gift. If you have more than one dog, however, make sure they are given bones well away from each other, as no matter how placid their nature, they will often fight tooth and nail over a bone.

Bathing your dog

It is not necessary to bath your dog more than once every four months. Unless you are taking him to a show or he has rolled in something unpleasant, his grooming sessions will be enough to keep his coat in good order. Often a good sponge with some warm water and then a quick drying session with a towel will suffice.

It is a good idea to clean your dog's teeth at least once a week to avoid plaque and prevent tartar building up. Use a special toothbrush and canine toothpaste.

Bathtime should never be stressful for either of you, so get your dog used to being in the bath from a young age and having the shower run over him. My dogs all love having a bath, even though I invariably end up getting almost as wet as they do.

Before you start, arm yourself with waterproofs, a robust sense of humour and some specially formulated dog shampoo (available from pet shops and good supermarkets). Lift your dog into the bath and make sure that you have a non-slip bath mat for him to stand on.

Wet his coat thoroughly with the shower, making sure you get under his tummy and down his legs. Rub in some shampoo, working up the suds all over his body. Leave his head until last, and shield his eyes with your hand to avoid any discomfort. Be especially careful not to get any water inside his ears.

Be sure to rinse his coat thoroughly, as shampoo residue can lead to flaking skin. If his coat is rinsed properly, you should be able to rub his hair vigorously without any sign of a lather.

Lastly, lift your dog out of the bath and stand well back, as he may decide to shake himself. Wrap him in a towel and then dry gently. Don't let him out, particularly on a cold day, until he is completely dry. Some dogs will tolerate being dried with a hair dryer, which speeds up the process.

Exercise

Staffords absolutely love exercise. Equal amounts of roadwork (walking on hard surfaces, such as pavements) and free running are ideal. When people ask me how much exercise they need to give their Stafford I usually tell them to do as much as they can manage – you will tire long before your dog does.

I walk my dogs in the morning for a minimum of half an hour, and then again in the evening for a minimum of an hour-and-a-half, or longer if the weather permits. The evening walk usually involves some free running. If you are unable to go out, let your dog run in the garden or take time to play with him and a favourite toy. Staffords rely on exercise for their mental as well as their physical well-being.

Remember that a Stafford will not exercise himself if you simply shut him outside on his own to do 20 laps of the garden – you need to be out there with

him. Always watch your dog if he is free running in a public place. Be aware of other dogs around him and take a ball or a toy which you can throw for him. This is not only an enjoyable game, but it also concentrates his mind wonderfully. My Staffords become oblivious to absolutely everything else if I have their favourite ball in my hand.

Running should be done for relatively short periods. A Stafford has a short muzzle and can be prone to becoming 'over-excited'. Use your common sense and if you find him snorting away after a run, put him back on his lead and walk for a while. Also, it is important to avoid too much free running on very hot days; the heat will not stop him from wanting to do it but he will soon get overheated and out of breath.

Always take a bottle of water on your walks. If your Stafford does become too hot, then let him have a drink from it. Dogs cool down quickly if you cool off their pads (the hard skin on the bottom of the feet). You can use the water to do this as well.

Be responsible

It probably goes without saying, but you should only let your Stafford off his lead if you are 100 per cent sure that you have full control over his actions. Bear in mind that his instinct is to naturally display aggression (not always, but it is better to be safe than sorry). If you are at all unsure, then keep him on the lead until you have a clear area to yourselves.

The law regarding dog fouling has recently undergone some changes, and

dog owners who don't clean up after their dogs in public places now face very heavy fines. Always take something with you on walks to clean up any mess that your dog makes – babies' nappy sacks are ideal as well as being scented.

Travelling with your dog

By the time he is an adult, your Stafford should be familiar with car travel. Unless your breeder, vet and training classes are all within walking distance, he will have already travelled in a car to or from them all at some time in his life.

It is always safer to put your dog in a crate whilst you are travelling. This can be placed on the back seat or – in an estate car or hatchback – in the back of the car. The crate will mean that the dog

Staffords love exercise and free-running. Don't allow your dog off the lead until you are sure you have full control over him.

is safe from harm and he will feel more secure. Alternatively you can now buy a special dog safety harness, which is designed to work much like a human seatbelt. The harness is attached to the dog and is then clipped into the car, often using the existing seatbelt clips to secure it.

If your dog is not accustomed to travelling in a car, it may be a good idea to have someone hold him on their knee to reassure him for his first couple of outings – cars can be frightening to dogs who are unused to them.

Never allow your dog to be loose when travelling by car. Not only is it

dangerous for him if you have to brake suddenly, but it endangers you, too, if he suddenly decides that he wants to sit on your knee and lick your ear whilst you are driving at 70 miles per hour along the motorway.

Crates are ideal for travelling. They fit in the back of most cars, even on the back seat if you don't have an estate car.

Travel sickness

If your dog has always travelled happily in the car without any problems, then it is very unlikely that he will succumb to car sickness. If he does seem to suffer with it, however, do not feed him a big meal before setting off on a journey. There are some effective remedies for canine car sickness, so consult your vet and ask for advice.

Note: It goes without saying that a dog should never ever be left in a car on a hot day, even with the windows down. Dogs can die agonising deaths by getting too hot in a car, so never risk it.

Going on holiday

If you go away on holiday, you may not be able to take your dog with you. However, there are plenty of holiday destinations, hotels, B & Bs and self-catering establishments that welcome dogs. You can even take your dog on holiday abroad under the Pet Passport scheme. Ask your vet or contact DEFRA for further information (see page 126).

If you are not taking your dog with you, the best thing is for a member of your family or a friend to look after him while you are away, either in their own home or in your house. However, they must be made fully aware of what this will entail and the extra pressure this will put on their time.

If you choose to leave your dog in a boarding kennel, you need to make sure that your Stafford's vaccinations are up to date, including his boosters. Most boarding kennels will not accept dogs whose vaccinations are out of date, in consideration for other dogs that may be staying at the same time. Visit the kennels beforehand and have a look round to check for cleanliness, helpful and knowledgeable staff – a good kennel will have no problem with this.

Remember to tell the staff of any special dietary needs your dog has: most kennels will charge less if you provide your dog's food. Take your dog's lead and a couple of his favourite toys with you when you drop him off. Try not to worry too much about leaving him – most Staffords are very adaptable creatures and they will quickly get used to their new surroundings.

The senior Stafford

One of the reasons I love this breed so much is that a senior citizen Stafford is often just as giddy as a puppy. However, we must all be realistic and understand that our dogs will age. It is important, therefore, to recognize the signs of ageing and alter the way we look after them to better suit their needs.

Ageing is a very gradual process in any mammal, so do not think that you will put a middle-aged dog to bed one night and wake up to find the Stafford version of Grandpa Simpson the following morning. My advice is to treat your Stafford like a puppy every day of his life until he decides otherwise.

Signs of ageing

If pressed to generalize on the lifespan of the breed, I would say that 13–14 years is average. The ever-youthful attitude of the Stafford means that, quite often, the first indication that your dog is getting on in years is a grey muzzle. Other signs that he may be approaching his free bus pass include the following:

- Deeper sleeping patterns together with a reluctance to bound out of his bed in the morning
- A gradual disinterest in his food, usually due to the fact that as he gets older, his sense of smell and taste become less acute
- His responses may get slower: if you call him he may appear to ignore you
- He may not be quite so eager to go out for his walks, although this usually means a leisurely stroll rather than not wanting to exercise at all.

Caring for seniors

As your Stafford lives out his twilight years, be aware that, unlike humans, he has no concept that he is getting older. His instincts to eat less, sleep more and generally turn slowly into a 'grumpy old man' will mean nothing to him on an intellectual level.

To this end, you need to make sure that you tailor his life accordingly, which will mean that his old age will be just as enjoyable as the rest of his life with you. His behaviour may also change as he ages, but this will be covered in the next chapter (see page 74).

Food

It is probably a good idea now to cut down the amount of food given in your dog's meals. Adding a little tasty gravy or the stock of a well-boiled bone to his food will help make it more palatable for him. Do not be tempted to offer him extra 'treats'. You may want him to be happy, but the fact is that as he ages he will tend to put on extra weight anyway,

and feeding unnecessary treats will only do him more harm than good.

Exercise

Your senior citizen may not enjoy – nor will he require – the same amount of exercise to which he was accustomed to as a youngster. Make his walk fun and turn back as soon as he has had enough. Look for warning signs, such as sitting down or walking very slowly behind you, as these will indicate that he has had enough and he wants to go home.

Do you need the vet?

In common with ageing humans, there may come a time when your only option is to consult your vet for professional advice. Any of the following should be considered worthy of a visit:
- Frequent accidents in the house
- Crying or whining during movement
- Total lack of interest in food
- Wobbly movement or rapid eye movement (this can suggest a stroke)
- Any changes in breathing patterns not associated with exercise
- Sudden changes in behaviour, e.g. aggression, listlessness or insomnia.

Time to say goodbye

The worst thing about owning a Stafford is having to let go. To lose a dog who epitomizes life and its enjoyment is never easy, but always keep in the back of your mind that you owe it to him to make the right decision in the end.

Your vet will never put your dog to sleep without first talking to you at length. No vet will destroy a dog who

Accidents

As he ages, your Stafford may – not will – have accidents in the house. This is just a result of an ageing and less efficient bladder. Try not to get cross with him – it won't make any difference – and, if the accident has occurred in the middle of the night or when you are not there, he will not understand what he is being told off for anyway.

shows even a minimal chance of survival with treatment. However, if your vet advises you that your Stafford's quality of life has diminished beyond medical help, you must be brave and recognize that it is time to let your dog go.

Euthanasia is a painless event and involves a dose of anaesthetic that will cause your dog's heart to stop beating. It is very peaceful and causes no distress or discomfort to your pet.

Staffords never lose their sense of fun, and even when they are senior citizens they will still enjoy spending time with you, playing games and having all their usual treats! Try to make their old age comfortable and fun.

Your vet will probably encourage you to stay with your dog during this quick procedure. However, if you find that this is too distressing, then don't put yourself through it. Just say goodbye and try not to let your Stafford see your distress.

Chapter 5

Behaviour

Recently we have seen the Stafford come under severe attack from the media. The public's perception of the breed as a dangerous, possibly lethal, machine is sad and extremely misguided. Any breed can be trained to attack and can suffer from inherent temperament problems, and therefore it is essential that, as custodians of this beautiful breed, we ensure this anti-dog trend is reversed.

As far as temperament goes, a good and well-bred Stafford is virtually bomb-proof. However, he must be well-trained, treated well and taught right from wrong. In this chapter, we will look at the behaviour of the breed and how to spot and stop any potential problems.

A matter of personality

In common with any living creature, it would be wrong to generalize when it comes to the personality of the Stafford. Some – perhaps the majority – are boisterous and fun loving; they have strong characters and are certainly not shrinking violets. They adore people and enjoy human company – particularly children – and they need plenty of physical and mental stimulation and a nutritious, well-balanced diet. Other dogs, however, may be quieter and more reserved, although any Stafford will behave like a clown given the chance.

One of the things I absolutely love about the breed is that it never seems to grow up. Staffords are as eager and happy to see you at 14 years of age as they are at 14 months. They love acting

Pack leader

The main point to get across to your dog is that you are the pack leader, and he will be more than happy to assume a more subservient role. There are several ways to do this, including the following:

• Make sure you walk through doors first; don't let him push through in front of you
• Do not allow him to get up on the sofa or your bed
• Ensure you initiate all activities, from walks to feeding times.

Opposite: Recent bad publicity in the media regarding the Stafford is untrue and unfair.

the fool and can be hilariously giddy. These traits are adorable, but do not expect a breed that will lie passively at your feet all day (though they do have moments of quiet reflection) – this is a demanding dog.

A happy breed

Staffords often appear to be smiling: their wide jaws and round eyes make them look constantly happy, a fact that is borne out by their clear love of life.

However, this smiling face does not mean that boundaries should not be set to make sure their behaviour remains acceptable. You must establish the ground rules of good behaviour:
• Try to avoid games where you tease your dog
• Ensure there are clear boundaries between playtime and downtime – you should always dictate these times, not your dog
• Don't play strength games unless you are going to win. Owing to the Stafford's giddy nature, it is very easy for tugging or swinging games to send him into a fit of utter stupidity. Always make sure you are in charge at times like this – if you feel he is getting out of hand, slow down and get him to sit down for a while.
• Don't work your dog up into a frenzy of excitement – he can be quite a handful and can easily forget his own strength
• Have fun with him – that's what he's there for – but be clear that playtime cannot be a 24-hour-a-day state of mind, for either of you.

I personally have found that bitches are slightly less 'fizzy' than male dogs and tend to be slightly quieter. However, I have also met plenty of bitches who are completely bonkers – in the nicest possible way. Remember that your Stafford will not think like you, no

Staffords love a game of 'tug', but it is very important to make sure that you are always in charge and it is you who 'wins'.

matter how much you wish he does; a dog is incapable of rational thought as we know it. Every dog is unique and it is far easier for you to 'think dog' than expect him to 'think human'.

Reprimanding your dog

All youngsters need reprimanding at some time of their lives. Without this, they would become wild and out of control with no idea that they were doing anything wrong. What you must remember with your dog is that a reprimand must *only* be given if you catch him in the act. Scolding a dog even 60 seconds after the deed has been done is pointless; he will not associate his punishment with the misdemeanour.

Similarly, you must not resort to the oft-recommended advice of 'rubbing his nose in it' if your puppy or adult dog has an accident indoors. This exercise is utterly pointless. The common expression that 'He looks guilty, so he knows what he's done' is also rubbish. Dogs do not feel guilt – their brains are not capable of doing so.

Be careful not to confuse fear with guilt: if your Stafford thinks he is going to be punished he will show fear, and a scared dog will never make a happy or reliable companion.

The use of the word 'No' in a firm voice will eventually be all that your dog will need in order to distinguish between acceptable and non-acceptable behaviour. Remember that the command will only work if you catch your Stafford red-handed in the act; it's a waste of your breath if you do it afterwards, and no

Making your Stafford wait patiently for a few moments before feeding him will show him that you are the pack leader.

amount of pointing at the puddle on the floor or the chewed trainer will make any difference to his understanding.

Early problems

'Problem' is not a word that anyone wants to see in relation to a Stafford. Indeed, perhaps it is the wrong word to use. However, there are some behaviours that you must watch out for in the early days, as the sooner they are dealt with the better. Always remember that your gorgeous baby will soon grow into one of the strongest breeds of dog, at which stage behavioural problems can be harder to rectify on your own.

Play biting or nipping

This is a common activity in any young dog, and your Stafford puppy will be no exception. Watch any puppy interact with his littermates (brothers and sisters) and you will notice that they 'play fight', which simply involves biting each other on various parts of the body. Watch long enough and you will see that if a bite hurts, the injured party will give a loud yelp. This mimics the cry of a human who has been hurt, and will be a great warning sign if your puppy does do something wrong.

In fact, this is the best way you can tell your puppy that he is hurting you. If he decides to play and sink his baby teeth into you, yelp loudly and he will soon learn to stop, even if he looks surprised at first. This will instill in him that biting is wrong, even in play.

Whining

Stafford puppies are wonderful whingers. Like a human baby, your new puppy will undoubtedly try his hand at crying to attract your attention. Do not get annoyed by this behaviour – remember that this is your Stafford's only way of communication at the moment and he is trying to tell you something.

Whining will usually happen at the beginning of your puppy's new life with you, often at night when you go to bed and he is alone in his crate.

This puppy is 'play-fighting' with his very patient mum! Don't let him play-bite you. If he gets rough, yelp loudly to make him stop.

To solve this problem, you need to let your puppy know that he is not alone and that he will see you soon. Fill his sleeping space with his favourite toys and a blanket, or a shirt that has your familiar smell on it. Sometimes leaving the television or a radio on is a good idea in the first couple of weeks.

Don't be tempted to take your puppy into your bedroom or bed at this stage. This will create future problems when he is a 20kg (44lb) adult who will not be able to understand why he cannot share your bed any more.

Digging

Dogs, particularly terriers, love digging. Their name is derived from the word

Like all terriers, Staffords like to dig and you may find several holes in the lawn or flower bed. A firm 'No' if he is caught in the act will eventually pay off.

'terrain', meaning ground, and you may find that your Stafford has decided to dig up parts of your garden. However, you can rule out the obvious reasons, such as boredom or the possibility that he has buried something there.

• If you catch your dog digging, use the command 'No'
• If you find a fresh hole, take him to it, point to it and use the same command
• If he really does just love digging, why not do what I do and designate an area of the garden and only allow him to dig there.

Begging

The number one rule with a dog who begs is never to give in. Most dogs will suddenly appear at the sound of a food packet being opened, or the rattle of a cutlery tray, because they associate these sounds with dinner. If you treat your dog just for appearing when there is food in the vicinity, you are actually rewarding this behaviour and telling him that begging is the kind of behaviour which will result in a treat. Children are the biggest culprits for feeding a begging dog, so make sure that they know not to 'share' their food with him.

The best way to deal with a 'beggar' is to simply ignore him. He will soon learn that this is a pointless exercise and realize that there will be no reward for his begging behaviour, no matter what he does, how beseechingly he looks at you, or how long he sits there.

Barking

I am touching wood as I say this, but I have never owned a Stafford whose barking became anything close to being a problem. However, if your dog is barking frequently and for no apparent reason, then you need to do something about it before it drives you – and possibly your neighbours – mad.

- Never shout at your dog for barking
- If he begins a barking session, bend down to his eye level and give the firm and familiar command 'No'. You must continue this religiously until he realizes you mean it
- Never give a treat to a barking Stafford to shut him up; it may make him quiet momentarily, but he will think you are rewarding him for barking, which will only make the behaviour worse.

Leaving your Stafford

We all have to leave our dogs 'home alone' at some point and this can sometimes lead to them suffering from what is known as 'separation anxiety'. You need to make your dog understand from an early age that he will not come to any harm when you leave the house.

- When your new puppy joins your household, jingle your car keys regularly whilst in the house – this will stop him associating the sound of keys with you leaving

We all have to leave our Staffords for short periods. Make sure your dog has something to occupy him whilst you are gone.

An occupied Stafford will rarely cause any problems if he is left alone for short periods.

- Never make a big fuss when you do leave him, as this gives him conflicting feelings. Play it low key
- If your Stafford does cause a fuss when you leave, don't be tempted to keep returning to try and 'settle' him
- Give him a treat before you go if you wish and make sure he is in, or has access to, his crate or bed, so you leave him in the place he feels most secure
- Never lock your dog in his crate if you are going to be away for a while, and make sure he has some toys to occupy him
- Don't leave anything around that you want to be chewed – he may have a go if he is left for too long
- If you are going out for the day and you cannot take him with you, ask a neighbour or friend – someone he is familiar with – to come round and keep him company for a while.

Eating faeces

This revolting habit has the tongue-twisting name of coprochagia, and should be discouraged immediately. There are various reasons why your Stafford may be tempted to eat his own (or other dogs') faeces: he may be hungry, he may be lacking in certain nutrients, his diet may be low in fibre, or he may just like the smell and taste of it. In order to tackle this habit, you must eliminate the above factors.

- Ensure he is getting enough food and it is nutritionally balanced
- Have your vet check him over to rule out any medical reason
- Make sure that your dog is not just doing it through boredom because he has nothing else to do.

If the behaviour continues regardless of the above:

- Always clean up after your dog
- If he does his business in the garden, do not leave it there
- If you clean up every few days, try using a repellant on the faeces, which will immediately put your dog off – Tabasco sauce, mustard or pepper are all effective
- Try distracting him if you catch him in the act
- If all else fails, you may have to consider muzzling him whilst he is in the garden
- Finally, don't shout at your dog for doing this – to him it's just a tasty treat.

Staffords and children

This should be the shortest section in this chapter, because your Stafford will adore your children unconditionally. However, it is still worth reading the following to make sure that your children are aware of certain 'ground rules' when it comes to the dog.

The dog's mouth

Don't allow your child ever to play with your dog's mouth. Firstly, it is unhygienic and, secondly, it can give the dog the wrong signals. In his mind, it will put him above the children in the 'pack' hierarchy and can lead to problems as he gets older.

Mine!

The dog's toys are his toys and the children's toys are theirs. Never allow your child to try and extract a toy from your dog's mouth. Despite the fact that I have watched my two-year-old wrestle a bone from a fully-grown male Stafford, it is best to avoid this.

Avoid tugging games

Staffords love tugging on things, and tug-of-war can be a great game with your dog and a piece of rope. However, whilst this is enjoyable with an adult who wins, never let your children attempt it. Not only is a Stafford very strong, but children often use eye contact in such games and some dogs may see this as confrontational.

Small masters

Make sure that your children are aware that their dog is not a toy and cannot be used as such. He is a member of the family and must be treated with respect and not teased or ill treated. A tragic true story that I am aware of involved a two-year-old Stafford bitch who was put to sleep after she bit a very young member of her family. On checking the bitch over later, the vet found that a pen had been shoved full length into her bottom – little wonder she nipped the child.

- Always include your children in any training you give to your dog. He should be in no doubt that even 'little' people are above him in the pecking order. They should use simple commands, such as 'Sit' and 'Stay'
- Don't forget that accidents can and do happen. Supervise your children at all times and use your own sense to allow them free time with your Stafford – they will all enjoy this immensely
- Take plenty of photographs of them all playing together – these memories will be precious to you in the future.

Lastly, I must stress that you should never leave a child alone with a Stafford (or any breed of dog for that matter), just to be on the safe side.

Aggression

An aggressive Stafford should always be considered a very serious problem. The breed's history, combined with his adult weight and strength, mean that any forms of aggression should be dealt with swiftly and decisively. Here, again, I must stress that this is true of any breed of dog – an aggressive Yorkshire Terrier, Great Dane or Poodle will pose exactly the same problems.

Basically, there are two main types of aggression: dog-to-human aggression and dog-to-dog aggression. If anything, your Stafford is more likely to display dog-to-dog aggression, which is mainly due to his inherent 'fighting dog' history. However, it can be controlled and it is not a great cause for concern.

As a responsible owner, it is essential that you stay in control of your dog at all times and you must make sure that you recognize and act on this behaviour should it arise.

Be sensible

There are some people who would tell you that any sign of aggression means an untrustworthy dog who can never be kept as a family pet. I cannot and would not condone aggressive behaviour in any dog, but you must make rational decisions. Most Staffords, for instance,

These young puppies are happy to play together with no outward signs of trouble.

will naturally display some form of aggression towards other dogs. In most cases, however, this behaviour can be modified sufficiently to allow you and your dog a happy and safe relationship.

Dog-to-dog aggression

Most cases of dog-to-dog aggression are the result of a natural and instinctive reflex in your Stafford to assert his dominance. Observe his behaviour when he is amongst other dogs. Does he look like he is trying to make himself tall? Does he prick up his ears? Does he puff out his chest? Watch his eyes. Does he maintain eye contact with the other dog? If the answer to any of these questions is 'Yes', then he is letting the other dog know that he is in charge.

No matter how loving and docile a temperament he has around his human family, a Stafford who displays a bad temperament around other dogs can cause problems. There can be several reasons why your dog is behaving like this, of which the most probable cause is that he feels threatened.

Dog-to-human aggression

This is going to be brief. A Stafford who shows aggression to humans is a major problem and you must deal with it promptly and decisively. However, it is extremely rare for this to affect the breed if you have brought your dog up to be sociable and relaxed around people of any age. If it is treated correctly, the behaviour can be remedied, so you need to act quickly.

- Never take this sort of aggression lightly or ignore it
- Seek professional help – you are strongly advised to speak to your vet who may advise a course of sessions with an animal behaviourist to identify the triggers for the aggressive behaviour and to find ways of preventing and curing it
- Never leave children or strangers alone with a potentially aggressive Stafford.

Do remember, however, that this type of behaviour is rare, and it is certainly not peculiar to the Stafford if it does occur.

A dog's aggression towards another dog is usually a direct result of insufficient socialization around other dogs at an early age. If you have taken him to socialization classes and out on a lead where other dogs have been in close proximity, it is unlikely that you will experience any problems. However, having attended more dog shows than I care to remember, I know only too well that Staffords really can be 'anti-dog'.

What to do

I always urge all Stafford owners to be ever-vigilant, as your dog, at some point, will probably 'have a go' at another dog. Your instinct will be to yank or pull roughly on his lead, although this may intensify the situation, as he will then feel even more threatened by the fact that he is being held back.

- Don't try and intervene between the two dogs – you could get bitten
- At the first sign of aggression, turn your Stafford around as swiftly as possible. Try not to use too much force, but make sure he knows you mean business
- Scold him as you pull him away and then praise him as soon as he is well away from the other dog – he will soon learn that aggression is not acceptable behaviour.

Senior moments

As he gets older, your Stafford may undergo changes in his behaviour. Vets and dog people usually quote the age of seven years as a rough guide to your dog becoming a veteran. Changes in behaviour can range from minor to major, so use your relationship and knowledge of him to tell you whether there are signs that you feel the vet should know about – your gut instinct will usually tell you. The following symptoms are not written in stone, but they can be exhibited in the senior dog:

- He may display a lack of interest in playtimes and/or exercise. Don't worry about this – it is normal. Instead of a two-mile walk, just take him for a one-mile amble
- If he tires chasing a ball, maybe he will be happy to chew a bone instead. He'll let you know what he would rather do
- He may sleep more than usual during the day
- He may look 'confused' with the sort of look on his face that we get when we walk into a room and forget why
- If partial loss of sight or hearing is apparent, he may appear unresponsive. Additionally, if he can't hear or see you approaching, his reaction may appear aggressive – the chances are you have given him a fright
- He will have less patience and may be more irritable.

Be patient with your Stafford if his behaviour does change slightly – he can not help it, he's just growing old and a bit grumpy in the same way as human senior citizens.

Be patient with your senior citizen and always ask your vet for advice if you feel concerned about his health and well-being.

Chapter 6

Showing and fun

Staffords make the ideal family pet and most owners will probably have chosen them for just that reason. However, a good specimen can also make a great showdog with his stunning looks and willingness to please. If you feel like trying your hand at showing your pedigree dog, the following is a step-by-step guide to how you go about it.

Ringcraft classes

Unless you want to make a complete idiot of yourself (and I'm talking from personal experience) make sure that you attend ringcraft classes with your Stafford before you enter any dog shows. These will teach you and him how to behave in the show ring, how to stack your dog (stand him in the show ring for the judge to assess) and how to move him correctly. You can find out about local classes in your area by checking with the Kennel Club (see page 126).

Types of show

There are various types of dog show, ranging from just a fun day out at an Exemption Show to the much more serious affair of the Championship Show, where the stakes are high and competition is fierce, perhaps with as many as 300 Staffords vying against each other for the top spot.

Exemption shows

These are fun shows that can be entered on the day. They are quite often held in conjunction with country shows or agricultural shows. They are the only type of show where registered pedigree dogs and cross-breeds can compete, and they are a great way to introduce your dog to the show ring.

General Open Shows

Hundreds of Open Shows are held throughout the UK every year. There will be many classes for you to enter, ranging from Puppy to Veteran. Open Shows are wonderful places to become initiated in the art of showing, learn the ropes and meet new friends. Most of these shows have classes for Staffords; if not, you can always enter the Any Variety Terrier classes.

Opposite: The Staffordshire Bull Terrier makes a stunning showdog, and you can have lots of fun as an exhibitor, especially if your dog enjoys showing and winning.

General Championship Shows

These are bigger than Open Shows and it is at a Championship Show that Challenge Certificates (CCs) may be on offer to the breed. A CC is an award given by the judge which will go towards making your Stafford a Champion. In a numerically large breed like the Stafford, it is no easy task to win a Challenge Certificate. A dog that wins three CCs under three different judges will become a Champion.

Championship shows are benched, which means that each dog will have a designated 'bench', somewhere safe where you can leave him in his crate or cage.

If your Stafford wins a first, second or third place at a Championship Show he will qualify for Crufts, which means that you will then be able to show him at the biggest dog show in the world.

Breed Club Shows

These are held by Staffordshire Bull Terrier Clubs countrywide and are open only to Staffords. They can be Open (no Challenge Certificates) or Championship (with Challenge Certificates). If you are a member of a Staffordshire Bull Terrier Club then you may also enter their Members and Limited shows. These are only open to paying members of the Club, so check with your local club on how to become a member. Be aware that there will be a small fee.

How to enter

Find out about the shows in your area by checking the canine press. *Our Dogs*

Make sure your dog is clean and well groomed before the show – bath him if necessary.

and *Dog World* are the UK's two 'dog' newspapers and they both contain advertisements for forthcoming shows in their classified sections. Remember that a puppy of less than six months old cannot be entered at a dog show.

What to do

1 Decide which shows you want to go to and then call the Secretary of the show to request a schedule. The Secretary's telephone number will appear on the show advertisement.

2 Check the schedule to find out which classes are available for your breed. These may be abbreviated, so be sure to check the schedule for definitions. Briefly, you may find Puppy (dogs of 6–12 months), Junior (dogs up to 18 months) or Open (any dog).

3 Decide which class(es) to enter and then fill in the form in the middle of the schedule. Remember to have your Stafford's pedigree to hand to make sure you spell his 'show name' correctly. You have to pay to enter your dog, which is more expensive at a Championship Show than an Open Show.

4 Send your completed 'entry', along with a cheque/postal order/credit card number, to the Secretary.

Note: Nowadays, you can enter some shows online – the show schedule will give you details.

The day of the show

Make sure that you set off in plenty of time, as there is nothing worse than arriving at a show as your class is being

Getting ready

- Make sure you have any passes for the show ready to take with you. These usually arrive a couple of weeks beforehand. They may be car park passes or vouchers for catalogues
- A few days before the show, you may wish to give your Stafford a bath – judges will mark down dirty dogs. However, if his coat is clean and fresh smelling, then a good brush and shine may be all that is needed
- Make sure that his collar and lead are clean – you can get special show collars for your Stafford which look particularly smart. Check with your local Stafford Club who will be able to help
- Check that your dog's crate or cage is clean. You will need to take this with you to house your Stafford at the show.

called. On arrival, you will be asked your name and, if you have prepaid for one, you will be given a catalogue. This will have the details of all the dogs who are entered at the show and which classes they are entered in.

Find a suitable place to put your cage or crate and then settle your dog down. I usually cover my Stafford's cage with a big blanket at shows, which prevents him becoming too distracted. Now you can just relax and sit back and wait for your class to be called.

In the ring

There are usually two officials in the ring – a steward (there may be two depending on how many dogs are entered) and a judge. The stewards will call out each class, so listen carefully for yours to be called. They will also tell you exactly where to stand in the 'line-up' and what to do, so don't worry if you have never been to a show before.

Try to relax. Always remember that nerves travel down the lead. If you feel stressed and nervous, then your dog will feel the same way, and an anxious dog will never show to his best advantage.

Be watchful in the ring for any signs

(Judges will assess your Stafford and see how well he fits the Kennel Club's Breed Standard.

of dog-to-dog aggression (see page 82). Several Staffords in close proximity to each other may want to exercise their superiority. The judge and other Stafford owners will be used to this, but keep a tight grip on your dog and anticipate any unwanted behaviour.

Strike a pose

Show Staffords are one of the few 'head' breeds, meaning that when they are exhibited at a dog show they are posed for the judge with their heads facing forwards, or towards, the judge. This is because one of the main characteristics of the breed is its wonderful head, so as exhibitors we present this part of our dog first to the judge. The rest of his body should look symmetrical, with both front legs in a straight line and the back legs level.

I start putting my Staffords in a 'show pose' from a young age. From about eight weeks old, I will stand them for about a minute, with one hand under their chin and my other hand gently supporting their tummy. This gets them accustomed to being handled and also to being told to 'Stand', which is the command I use for this exercise. If you want to show your Stafford, it will pay dividends to start early on.

Judges need to be able to assess your dog by placing their hands on various parts of him. They will check his head, teeth, stop, back, undercarriage, tail, legs and testicles (unless you are showing a bitch). Judges need to do this to make

Make sure you never put yourself between your dog and the judge whilst moving him. You can practise this at ringcraft classes.

Get your Stafford used to having his mouth handled and his teeth looked at from the earliest possible age.

sure that your dog's construction fits the Breed Standard, and that his coat is clean and his teeth are correct.

Firstly, the judge will walk up and down the ring in order to get an overall impression of all the dogs. He/she may walk in front, behind and to the side of your dog. Keep your Stafford as still as you can while this happens (they love being tickled under the tummy and it always makes mine stand still).

It's your turn

When it is your Stafford's turn to be judged, you will be asked by the steward to get your dog stacked for the judge. Try and stay focused on your dog and the judge, and do not watch what

everyone else is doing – this is your big moment. Make as little fuss as possible. The judge will not talk to you apart from asking your dog's age. Reassure your dog as the judge assesses him. If he moves, simply place his feet back in position.

The judge will now 'go over' your dog. He will perform a full assessment on him, including checking his teeth, ears, tail, feet and overall conformation. He does this to find out how closely your Stafford compares to the Kennel Club Breed Standard. When he is happy with his 'hands-on' examination, you will be asked to move.

On the move

The judge is likely to ask you to move your dog in a straight line (away from him and then towards him), followed by a triangle (away, across and then back towards). He does this to assess the way your Stafford is moving going away, coming towards and in side gait.

One golden rule is to never allow yourself to come between the dog and the judge. If your Stafford acts up, just stop and set off again; no judge will have a problem with this. You have paid your money for their opinion and judges always want you to do your best.

Crunch time

When the judge has assessed all the exhibits, a decision will be made. Watch the judge carefully in case you are asked to move your dog again, or they want to check him over for a second time. The judge will place the first three to five dogs and will thank everyone else for their time and participation.

If you have been placed, stay in the ring. You will be awarded your rosette and the judge will want to do a written critique on your dog, which will then be submitted to the canine press for publication. If you don't happen to get placed, don't worry – just remember the exhibitors' motto: you always take the best dog home.

Staffords are doing increasingly well in the discipline known as Agility.

Agility

Agility is a canine discipline which is fun, easy to do and is gaining popularity amongst Stafford owners. In fact, over the last couple of years, the breed has proved extremely adept at this training practice. Friends with Staffords who go to Agility classes claim that their dogs really enjoy the physical and mental stimulation it affords them.

You will most probably have seen this displayed and televized at Crufts dog show. A course is set for the dogs,

Ring manners

Even dog shows have an unofficial code of conduct, or ring etiquette if you like. The following guidelines may be helpful:

- Never talk to the judge in the ring. You may be asked your dog's age, but this will probably be the only time you speak to your judge. It is not acceptable to question a judge in the ring, and if you are eager to find out what they thought of your dog, politely ask them outside the ring on completion of judging
- Never shout to your family or friends outside the ring. This is rude to other exhibitors and off-putting to the judge
- Don't leave the ring until you have been told to do so by the steward
- Whether you agree with their choices or not, remember that the judge is in charge of the ring and their decision is final.

including jumps, tunnels, slaloms and other obstacles. The idea is to navigate the course with your Stafford – you don't have to jump through the hoops though! Points are awarded or deducted for the length of time it takes, any faults and on how well the obstacles have been tackled.

It is recommended that Staffords are not introduced to Agility until they are at least 12 months of age. If you are interested in Agility, contact the Kennel Club or your breed club for classes in your area (see page 126).

The Good Citizen Scheme

This is a wonderful scheme that was set up by the Kennel Club, whereby dogs can win Gold, Silver and Bronze awards for being, literally, good citizens. Your Stafford will be judged on a number of good behaviour tests. Many shows now include the chance to enter the GCDS. I personally love to see our breed take part in these, as it shows people what remarkable and well behaved dogs they

really are. You can contact the Kennel Club for further details (see page 126).

Participating in the Kennel Club's Good Citizen Dog Scheme gives you a chance to show off your Stafford's good behaviour.

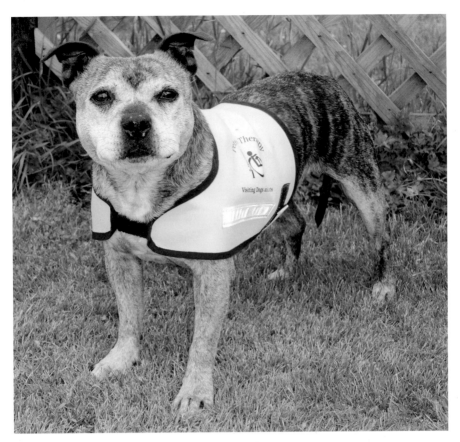

Many Staffords are now PAT (Pets As Therapy) dogs visiting elderly, hospitalized and disabled people. It is rewarding for you and your dog.

Heelwork to Music

As its name suggests, this combines obedience with your favourite tunes. In fact, it's not dissimilar to aerobic or dance classes for humans. Whilst I have only ever seen one Stafford take part in this discipline, it is fun, but be prepared for your friends to laugh at you. If you are interested in Heelwork to Music, contact the Kennel Club or your breed club for details of classes in your area (see page 126).

Obedience

Staffords have come to the fore in Obedience, the basics of which you will already be familiar with. Obedience competitions are open to any breed and can be fun for both you and your dog. To get started join a local dog training club. These clubs focus on things such as recall (similar to getting your dog to come to you); heelwork (training him to walk to your left heel) and retrieving (bringing objects back to you). For shows that offer obedience classes, contact the Kennel Club (see page 126).

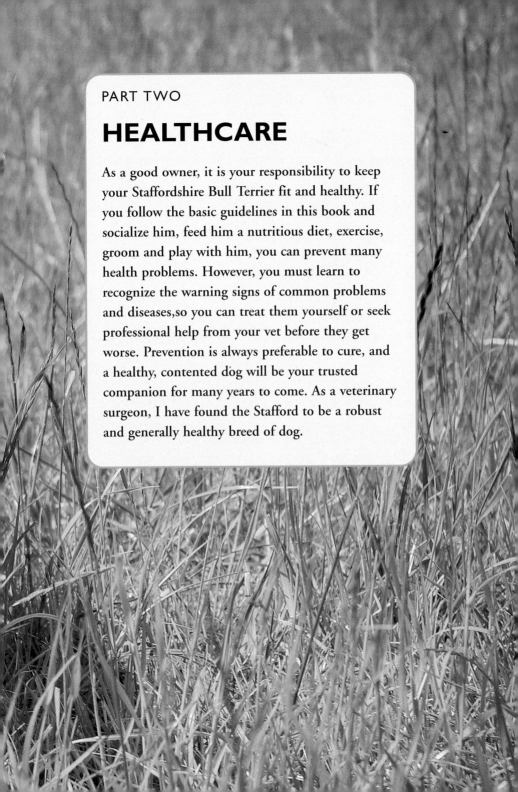

PART TWO

HEALTHCARE

As a good owner, it is your responsibility to keep
your Staffordshire Bull Terrier fit and healthy. If
you follow the basic guidelines in this book and
socialize him, feed him a nutritious diet, exercise,
groom and play with him, you can prevent many
health problems. However, you must learn to
recognize the warning signs of common problems
and diseases,so you can treat them yourself or seek
professional help from your vet before they get
worse. Prevention is always preferable to cure, and
a healthy, contented dog will be your trusted
companion for many years to come. As a veterinary
surgeon, I have found the Stafford to be a robust
and generally healthy breed of dog.

Signs of good health

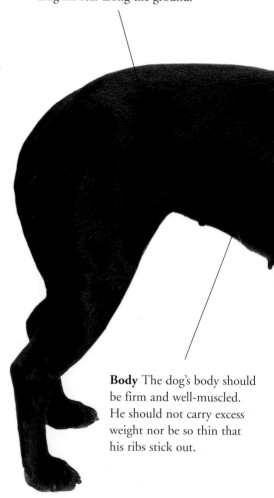

Anal region This should be clean without any faeces clinging to the fur. The dog should not lick this area excessively or drag his rear along the ground.

Body The dog's body should be firm and well-muscled. He should not carry excess weight nor be so thin that his ribs stick out.

Eyes The eyes should be bright, alert and with no signs of discharge, swelling or tear stains. A tiny amount of 'sleep' in the inner corners is quite normal.

Ears They should be responsive to any sound. The insides should be pale pink with no visible wax or unpleasant smell. Your dog should not shake his head or scratch his ears too often.

Nose The nose of a healthy dog should be cold and damp without any discharge. Occasionally there may be a little clear fluid.

Teeth Healthy teeth are white and smooth, not yellow, which can be a sign of plaque and tartar formation. The breath should not smell unpleasant and there should be no loose or missing teeth or inflamed or bleeding gums.

Claws The claws should end level with the pad and not be too long. Look out for broken claws, damage to dew claws (if they have not been removed) and hay seeds embedded in the pads.

Hereditary diseases

As in humans, dogs can inherit a wide range of diseases. They are caused by genetic faults or aberrations in the breeding line. Staffords are basically very healthy dogs and are heir to fewer hereditary diseases than many other breeds. Where they do occur, they tend to affect only certain blood lines.

Genetic faults

The genetic background to many hereditary ailments can be extremely complicated. Screening tests are available for tendencies to some hereditary diseases, and potential owners of dogs, particularly pedigrees, should consult their vet about possible inherited health problems within the breed and ask the breeder about the lineage and history of the dams and sires before purchasing a puppy. Although some hereditary diseases are treatable, the underlying genetic faults cannot be eliminated.

Hip dysplasia

This is one of the most common inherited diseases and affects many breeds. The Staffordshire Bull Terrier breed is not particularly prone to it, but it does occur in some blood lines. In a normal, healthy dog the hip is a 'ball and socket' joint, allowing a wide range of movement. The rounded end at the top of the femur fits tightly into the cup-shaped socket in the pelvis. In hip dysplasia, a shallow socket develops with a distorted femur head and slack joint ligaments. There can be excessive movement between the femur and pelvis, leading to a malfunctioning joint which will gradually become arthritic.

Early symptoms

If a puppy develops severe hip dysplasia he may have difficulty walking. Getting up from a sitting position may be painful and he will cry out. When he runs, he may use both hind legs together in a 'bunny hop' or look as though he is swaying. These symptoms may be identifiable from five months onwards. Mildly affected puppies may show no signs at all of hip dysplasia at this age, but they will begin to develop arthritis at about eight years of age.

Hip dysplasia scheme

The British Veterinary Association and the Kennel Club run a joint scheme (the BVA/KC hip dysplasia scheme) based on hip scoring. The vet submits the X-ray, bearing the KC registration number of the dog, to the scheme. Each hip is then scored from 0 to 54, making a total of 108 maximum between the two hips. The lower the score the better, and 0:0 is the best score possible.

You should not breed from a dog or bitch with a higher hip score than the average for the breed or hip dysplasia will never be reduced or eliminated from that breed. When buying a puppy, check that both parents have been X-rayed, scored, and achieved a low score. This does not guarantee he won't develop hip dysplasia but it does reduce the chances.

Treatment

If mild hip dysplasia is treated in a growing puppy with anabolic steroids, limited exercise and diet, he will often grow into a healthy adult dog. However, you may have to restrict his exercise later on, too. In severe cases, surgery is available.

Other hereditary conditions

The most important hereditary diseases of Staffords are so-called L-2-HGA and certain eye conditions.

L-2-HGA

This is an uncommon disease of the dog's metabolic processes. It has been diagnosed in totally unconnected blood lines and the number of cases seems to be gradually rising. Symptoms can be highly variable and include tremors, unsteady gait, muscle stiffness, seizures and behaviour changes, such as episodes of anxiety and dementia. First signs of the condition usually appear at between six months and one year of age but can come later. For a dog to be affected, both parents must carry the gene responsible for the condition. A genetic test is now available for the detection of L-2-HGA carriers. There is, as yet, no specific cure and the vet can only advise on palliative, symptomatic treatment.

Eye diseases

Staffordshire Bull Terriers are predisposed to some eye diseases. These include cataracts in the lenses of both eyes, juvenile cataracts developing in young puppies and – sorry about the long scientific names – persistent hyperplastic vitreous and persistent hyperplastic tunica vasculosa lentis.

In the two latter conditions, which are hereditary, tissues that existed in the embryonic eye fail to disappear when the eye fully develops and go on to damage the lens with the resultant formation of cataracts and sometimes result later in blindness. Ophthalmic surgery will help in some cases, but preventive measures, in the form of selective breeding that excludes severely affected dogs, are preferable. Dogs can now be screened for hereditary cataract by means of a DNA test as well as traditional ophthalmoscopy. The other eye conditions mentioned can be detected by screening by a veterinary ophthalmologist from six weeks of age.

Entropion

In this inherited eye disease, the edge of the eyelid folds inwards so the lashes rub against the eyeball itself. The eye becomes sore and weeps and may be kept closed. The condition can be corrected, however, with surgery.

Cleft lip and cleft palate

Important surgical conditions to which Staffords are prone are cleft lip and cleft palate. The cause in some cases may be genetic. In others, excessive Vitamin A intake in the form of too much liver, too much cod liver oil, too many vitamin supplements during pregnancy, the administration of cortisone-type drugs during pregnancy, or the cytotoxic drug hydroxyurea seem to be responsible. Treatment by surgery as soon as the condition is recognized is recommended.

Preventing disease

Prevention is always better than cure, and there is a lot you can do as an owner to prevent diseases and health problems developing by keeping your dog in first-class condition. Get into the habit of inspecting and looking after his ears, eyes, teeth, coat, paws and rear end.

Check your dog

You should check your dog on a regular basis – a grooming session is always a good opportunity to examine him.

1 Look inside your dog's mouth, checking that his teeth are clean and white and that his breath does not smell unpleasant. Clean the teeth with specially formulated toothpaste at least once a week.

2 Next, check his eyes, nose and ears for signs of any discharge, odour or inflammation. You can keep them clean by wiping them gently with some damp cotton wool.

3 Examine the dog's coat, parting the hairs and looking for any bald patches, excessive hair loss, tell-tale signs of fleas (black sooty specks in the fur) and any soiling around the anus and rear end. The coat should always look healthy and glossy, and the dog should not scratch excessively.

4 Pick up each of your dog's paws and check the pads and claws, which should not be broken nor too long. If your dog appears to be limping, look for cuts or any swellings on the pads. Some dog breeds are susceptible to grass and hay seeds becoming embedded in their pads.

Note: If you find anything unusual or suspect there may be a health problem, then make an appointment to take your dog to the vet. Even if it is only a minor worry, this will set your mind at rest. You can treat the problem before it gets more serious and learn how to prevent it recurring in the future.

Vaccinations

The most important thing that you can do to protect your dog's health is to make sure that he is vaccinated against the major infectious canine diseases. These are distemper, infectious canine hepatitis, 'kennel cough', parvovirus and the two forms of leptospirosis.

Vaccination against all these serious ailments can be given by your vet in one shot when your puppy is at least six weeks of age. A second dose will be administered three to six weeks later. An annual booster dose is recommended thereafter in order to top up your dog's immunity, although some veterinary authorities believe this is not necessary. However, like most vets, I personally am in favour of it.

In addition, in some countries the vaccination of dogs against rabies is obligatory. Puppies can be vaccinated as early as four weeks of age. Yearly booster shots are essential.

Pet Passports

If you are considering taking your dog on holiday to one of the European Union countries or to certain other designated rabies-free countries, you must obtain a Pet Passport. The same applies to dogs travelling abroad to dog shows and competitive events.

Your vet and the local DEFRA office will give you information on how to go about this. Your dog will have to be micro-chipped, vaccinated against rabies and blood tested 30 days after the vaccination before you leave for your trip, and then treated against ticks and other parasites 24 to 48 hours before your return with a veterinary certificate to prove it. You must have a DEFRA PETS re-entry certificate certifying that the blood test gave a positive result for immunity against rabies after the vaccination, and must sign a declaration that the dog did not leave the qualifying countries while you were away.

Neutering your dog

Unless you are definitely contemplating breeding from your dog, it is best, for the dog and for you, to have a bitch spayed or a dog castrated after she/he reaches six months of age. Castration reduces aggressiveness and the likelihood of a dog going a-roaming. Spaying, apart from avoiding the arrival of unwanted puppies, reduces the chances of breast tumours in later life and, obviously, the onset of common uterine disease, such as pyometra. Neither castration nor spaying change the character of dogs nor necessarily make them put on weight. Talk to your vet about what is involved.

Diet is important

Feeding a balanced and nutritious diet will help to keep your dog healthy. It is important not to over-feed him or he may gain too much weight and this can lead to many health problems that are associated with obesity as well as a reduced life expectancy.

If you are unsure as to which foods, how much and how often to feed your dog, ask your vet for advice. Similarly, if your dog loses his appetite or sheds weight suddenly, ask your vet's advice – the dog may well need worming (see page 105) or the symptoms may be a sign of a more serious problem.

Keep your dog fit and active

All dogs need regular exercise every day to keep them fit and stay in optimum health. The amount and type of exercise will vary according to the breed. Thus an active breed like the Staffordshire Bull Terrier should trot at least a mile or two every day, on the lead if in town or free running on open ground in parks or the countryside, in order to stay in prime condition. Try to get into the habit of walking your dog at least twice a day.

Stimulate your dog

Playing games with your dog in the house or garden and teaching him tricks will provide both mental and physical stimulation. Lively dogs like Staffords need to be busy and active, or they will soon become bored and this can lead to various behaviour problems as well as to poor health. So make time for your dog and play with him every day, preferably in several short sessions.

Parasites

Dogs can play host to two sorts of unwelcome parasite: external and internal ones. By worming your dog regularly and treating him with flea treatments, especially in the spring and summer, you can prevent infestations occurring and keep him healthy.

External parasites

These parasites live on the surface of the dog's body, and include lice, fleas, ticks, mites (see page 115) and ringworm (see page 116). Keep a look out for them and treat an infected dog as soon as possible.

Fleas

Dogs are usually infested by their own and the cat's species of flea but sometimes they can carry rabbit, human or hedgehog fleas. The infestations are more likely to be worse in warm weather in the summer, but fleas thrive all the year round, particularly if your home has central heating. Sometimes it is extremely difficult to find any fleas on a dog, but just a single flea can cause an allergic reaction when piercing a dog's skin and injecting its saliva. Such a reaction can result in widespread irritation, skin sores and rashes. Flea eggs

do not stick to the dog's hair like those of lice (see below), but, being dry, they drop off onto carpets and furniture.

What you can do Use insecticidal sprays, shampoos or powders, which are obtainable from the vet, chemist or a pet shop, at regular intervals throughout the summer. Treat the floors, furniture and your pet's favourite sleeping places, basket and bedding with a specially formulated aerosol product every seven months. This procedure effectively stops the re-infestation of dogs by larvae emerging from eggs in the environment.

Lice

There are two kinds: biting lice which feed on skin scales; and sucking lice which draw tissue fluids from the skin. The latter cause more irritation to the dog than the former. Lice are greyish-white and about 2mm (⅛in) in length. Their eggs (nits) are white and cemented to the dog's hairs. The dog louse does not fancy humans or cats and will not infest them.

> **COMMON SYMPTOMS**
> • An affected dog will keep scratching
> • Tiny reddish scabs or papules appear on the skin, particularly on the dog's back
> • Flea droppings look like coal dust in the coat.

> **COMMON SYMPTOMS**
> • The dog will scratch himself
> • Lice and nits will be visible to the naked eye when the dog's coat is carefully searched.

What you can do Sprays, powders or baths are available from the vet or pet shop. Apply on at least three occasions at five- to seven-day intervals to kill adults and the larvae that hatch from the nits.

Ticks
More often seen on country dogs than town dogs, ticks suck blood, their abdomen swelling up as they do so. The commonest tick of dogs is the sheep tick. It clings to the dog's hair, generally on the legs, head or under-belly, and pierces the skin with its mouth parts. In doing so it can transmit an organism called Borrelia, a cause of Lyme Disease. Characterized by lameness and heart disease, it requires veterinary diagnosis by means of blood tests, and then treatment using specific antibiotics and anti-inflammatory drugs.

What you can do Remove a tick by dabbing it with some alcohol, such as gin or methylated spirits, waiting a few minutes for its head to relax, and then grasping it near to the mouthparts with fine tweezers – you can buy special ones (see left). Dislodge the tick with a little jerk. Do not ever pull it off, however, without applying the alcohol first as the mouthparts left in the skin may cause an abscess to form.

An alternative method is to spray the tick with some flea spray and then to remove it the following day. The regular application of a flea spray or fitting your dog with an insecticidal collar during the summer months is highly recommended in order to control tick infestation.

Internal parasites
These parasites live inside the dog's body. Several kinds of worm can infest dogs

and, in very rare cases, these parasites can spread to human beings.

Roundworms
These live, when adult, in the dog's intestines but their immature forms migrate through their host's body, damaging such organs as the liver and lungs, particularly those of puppies.

Hookworms and whipworms
These blood-sucking parasites can cause severe anaemia. Your veterinary surgeon will be able to confirm if your dog is affected.

Tapeworms and roundworms
The commonest dog tapeworm, *Dipylidium*, is spread by fleas, in which its larvae develop. You can see the segments of this tapeworm looking like wriggling white grains of rice in droppings or stuck to the hair around the dog's bottom. Roundworms cause the most trouble for dogs, particularly puppies.

COMMON SYMPTOMS
- Symptoms of roundworms include bowel upsets, emaciation, fits, chest and liver malfunction
- Tapeworms may cause dogs to drag their rear ends ('scoot') along the floor.

What you can do To treat roundworms you should give your dog a 'worming' medication which will be available from your vet. Puppies usually should receive their first dose at three weeks of age. Repeat the worming every three weeks until they are 16 weeks old, repeating at six months and twice a year thereafter. Ask your vet for advice.

Give your dog anti-tapeworm medication once a year or when any worm segments are seen in his droppings or on the hair near and around the anus.

Regular flea control will also help you to combat tapeworms. Some worm treatments are effective against all types of internal parasites, and you should consult your veterinary surgeon about which products are suitable and the correct dosage.

Dental care

Check your dog's teeth regularly and brush them once or twice a week to prevent any tartar building up. Gnawing on a variety of bones and chews will help keep his teeth clean and healthy.

Tooth disease

It is relatively easy to spot the common symptoms of tooth disease and dental decay. They are listed below.

> **COMMON SYMPTOMS**
> • **Your dog may salivate (slavering) at the mouth**
> • **He may paw at his mouth**
> • **His chewing motions may be exaggerated**
> • **He may chew tentatively as if he is dealing with a hot potato**
> • **His breath may smell unpleasant.**

What you can do Cleaning the teeth once or twice weekly with cotton wool or a soft toothbrush dipped in salt water (or specially formulated dog toothpaste) will stop tartar formation. 'Bones' and 'chews' made of processed hide (available from all good pet shops) together with the occasional meal of coarse-cut, raw butcher's meat also helps.

Tartar

When tartar, a yellowy-brown, cement-like substance, accumulates, it does not produce holes in the teeth that need filling. Instead it damages the gum edge, lets in bacteria to infect the tooth sockets and thus loosens the teeth. Tartar always causes some gum inflammation (gingivitis) and frequently bad breath. If your pet displays the symptoms described, open his mouth and look for a foreign body stuck between his teeth. This may be a sliver of wood or bone stuck between two adjacent molars at the back of the mouth or a bigger object jammed across the upper teeth against the hard palate. You can usually flick out foreign bodies with a teaspoon handle.

Gingivitis

Bright red edging to the gums where they meet the teeth, together with ready bleeding on even gentle pressure, are the principal signs of gingivitis (gum disease). Tap each tooth with your finger or a pencil. If there are any signs of looseness or tenderness, wash the dog's mouth with some warm water and salt, and give him an aspirin tablet – there is little else you can do without seeking professional help. Take the dog to the vet and ask his advice.

Broken teeth

Sometimes a dog will break a tooth, perhaps by fighting or chewing stones (a bad habit that some dogs get into). The large 'fang' teeth (canines) are most often the ones damaged. These injuries do not usually produce any signs of toothache, root infection or death of the tooth. Treatments used in human dentistry, such as fillings, root treatments or crowning, may be necessary and they are all possible.

Ulcers and tumours

Mouth ulcers, tumours (juvenile warts are common in young dogs) and tonsillitis will all need veterinary diagnosis and treatment where they are the cause of some of the symptoms mentioned above.

Canine dentistry

This is easily tackled by your vet. Using tranquillizers or short-acting general anaesthetics, tartar can be removed from a dog's teeth with scrapers or an ultra-sonic scaling machine.

Antibacterial drugs may be prescribed if any encroaching tartar has caused secondary gum infection. Bad teeth must be taken out to prevent root abscesses and socket infection from causing problems, such as septicaemia, sinusitis or even kidney disease, elsewhere in the dog's body.

Eye problems

Your dog's eyes are precious and you must check regularly that they are normal and healthy.

COMMON SYMPTOMS
- Sore, runny or 'mattery' eyes
- Blue or white film over the eye
- Partially or totally closed eye or eyes.

Watering and discharge

If just one of the dog's eyes is involved and the only symptom is watering or a sticky discharge without any marked irritation, you can try washing the eye gently with boracic acid powder in warm water once every few hours, followed by the introduction of a little Golden Eye ointment (which is obtainable from the chemist) onto the affected eyeball. If any symptoms in or around the eyes last for more than a day, you must take the patient to the veterinary clinic and get professional treatment. Particularly in young dogs, two mattery eyes may indicate distemper (see page 110).

Eye conditions

Persistent watering of one or both eyes can be due to a very slight infolding of the eyelid (see opposite), or to blocked tear ducts. A blue or white film over one or both eyes is normally a sign of keratitis, which is an inflammation of the cornea. This is not a cataract but it does require immediate veterinary attention. Opacity of the lens (cataract) can be seen as a blue or white 'film' much deeper in the eye. The pupil looks greyish in colour instead of the usual black. This usually occurs in elderly dogs but it may be seen sometimes in young puppies (congenital cataract) and also at other ages (diabetic cataract).

Inflammations of the eye

These can be treated by the veterinarian in a variety of ways. Antibiotic injections, drops and ointments are available, plus various other drugs to reduce inflammation, as are surgical methods of tackling ulcerated eyes under local anaesthesia. Problems due to deformed eyelids, foreign bodies embedded in the eyeball and even some cataracts can all be treated surgically nowadays.

Ear problems

A healthy dog's ears should be alert and responsive to sounds. The ear flaps of most breeds are usually pale pink and silky inside, and there should be no wax or nasty odour. A dog who keeps scratching his ears and shaking his head may have an ear infection.

COMMON SYMPTOMS
- **Shaking the head and scratching the ear**
- **It is painful when the ear is touched**
- **There may be a bad smell and discharge**
- **The dog tilts his head to one side**
- **There is ballooning of the ear flap.**

Preventing problems

Clean your dog's ears once a week. For breeds with hair growing in the ear canal, pluck out the hair between finger and thumb. Don't cut it. Using 'baby buds' or twists of cotton wool moistened in warm olive oil, clean the ear with a twisting action to remove excess brown ear wax. See the vet early with any ear trouble. Chronic ear complaints can be very difficult to eradicate.

Treating minor problems

If symptoms suddenly appear and the dog is in distress, an effective emergency treatment is to pour a little warmed (not hot) liquid paraffin carefully into the affected ear. Acute inflammation will be greatly soothed by the oil. Don't stuff proprietary liquids into a dog's ear; you do not know what you may be treating. Most of all, avoid those so-called canker powders as the powder bases of these products can cause additional irritation by forming annoying accumulations that act as foreign bodies.

Ear irritation

This may be due to various things that find their way into the ear canal. Grass awns may need professional removal. Small, barely visible white mange mites that live in dog's ears cause itching, and bacteria can set up secondary infections. Sweaty, dirty conditions provide an ideal opportunity for germs to multiply. The vet will decide whether mites, bacteria, fungi or other causes are the source of inflammation, and will use antiparasitic, antibiotic or antifungal drugs as drops or injections.

Middle-ear disease

Although tilting of the head may be due simply to severe irritation on one side, it can indicate that the middle ear, the deeper part beyond the eardrum, is involved. Middle-ear disease does not necessarily result from outer-ear infection but may arise from trouble in the Eustachian tube which links the middle ear to the throat. This will always require some rigorous veterinary attention with the use of antiflammatory drugs, antibiotics and, more rarely, deep drainage operations.

Ballooning of an ear flap

This may look dramatic and serious but in fact it is a relatively minor problem. It is really a big blood blister, which is caused by the rupture of a blood vessel in the ear flap. It generally follows either some vigorous scratching where ear irritation exists or a bite from another dog. It can be treated surgically by the vet, who may drain it with a syringe or open it and then stitch the ear flap in a special way to prevent any further trouble.

Nose problems

Don't allow your dog's nostrils ever to get caked and clogged up. Bathe them thoroughly with warm water and anoint the nose pad with some soothing cold cream. If there are any 'common cold' symptoms, you must seek veterinary advice immediately.

> ### COMMON SYMPTOMS
> - **The dog's nostrils are running and mattery**
> - **The dog appears to have the equivalent of a human common cold**
> - **The nose tip is sore, cracked and dry**
> - **Check the eyes as well as the nose – if they are both mattery, the dog may have distemper.**

Sore noses

Old dogs with cracked, dry nose pads need regular attention to keep their nostrils free and to deal with bleeding from the cracks. Bathe the nose frequently, applying cod liver oil ointment twice or three times daily and working it in well.

Rhinitis and sinusitis

Sneezing, a mattery discharge from the nostrils, head shaking and, perhaps, nose bleed may indicate rhinitis (the inflammation of the nasal passages) or sinusitis (inflammation within one or more of the sinus chambers in the skull). Bacterial, viral or fungal germs, foreign bodies, growths, tooth abscesses or eye disease can be the cause.

Like humans, dogs possess air-filled spaces in the bones of their skulls (sinuses) which can become diseased. Infections or tumours can occur in these cavities. Sometimes an infection can spread into them from a bad tooth root nearby. The signs of sinusitis include sneezing, persistent nasal discharge and head shaking. If you notice these symptoms, take your dog to the vet. The treatment can involve anti-bacterial or anti-fungal drugs, surgical drainage or dental work as appropriate.

Respiratory problems

Dogs can suffer from bronchitis, pleurisy, pneumonia, heart disease and other chest conditions. Coughing and sneezing, the signs of a 'head cold', possibly together with mattery eyes, diarrhoea and listlessness, may indicate distemper – a serious virus disease.

> **COMMON SYMPTOMS**
> • **The dog may cough**
> • **There may be some wheezing and sneezing**
> • **The dog's breathing may be laboured.**

Distemper

Although this is more common in younger animals, it can occur at any age and shows a variety of symptom combinations. Dogs catching distemper can recover although the outlook is serious if there are symptoms such as fits, uncontrollable limb twitching or paralysis, which suggest that the disease has affected the nervous system. These may not appear until many weeks after the virus first invades the body.

What you can do Your dog should be vaccinated against distemper at the first opportunity – when he is a puppy – and do make sure that you keep the annual booster dose going. At the first signs of any generalized illness, perhaps resembling 'flu' or a 'cold', contact the vet. Keep your dog warm, give him plenty of liquids and provide easily digestible nourishing food.

Your vet will be able to confirm whether the dog has distemper. Because it is caused by a virus, the disease is very difficult to treat. Antibiotics and other drugs are used to suppress any dangerous secondary bacterial infections. Vitamin injections will help to strengthen the body's defences. The debilitating effects of coughing, diarrhoea and vomiting are countered by drugs which reduce these symptoms.

Coughs

Where troublesome coughs occur in the older dog, give him a half to two codeine tablets three times a day, depending on the animal's size. However, you should still take him to see the vet.

Heart disease

This is common in elderly dogs and often responds well to treatment. Under veterinary supervision, drugs can give a new lease of life to dogs with 'dicky' hearts. It is useful in cases of heart trouble and in all older dogs to give vitamin E in the synthetic form (50–200mgm per day depending on the dog's size) or as wheat germ oil capsules (two to six per day).

Bronchitis

Inflammation of the tubes that conduct air through the lungs can be caused by a variety of bacteria and viruses, parasitic lungworms, allergy, inhalation of dust, smoke, foreign bodies or even by excessive barking.

Specific therapy is applied by the vet and sometimes, in the case of foreign bodies, surgery or the use of a fibre-optic bronchoscope is necessary.

Pneumonia

There are many causes of pneumonia in dogs, the commonest being infections by micro-organisms such as viruses or bacteria. Migrating parasitic worm larvae and inhalation of foreign bodies are less frequent. The signs are faster and/or more laboured breathing, a cough, raised temperature and, often, nasal discharge. It can be treated with antibiotics, corticosteroids, 'cough' medicines and medication to relieve symptoms. Pneumonia always demands immediate professional attention.

Kennel cough

This is caused either by a bacterium (*Bordetella*) or viruses (Canine parainfluenza virus, Canine herpes virus or Canine adenovirus) or a mixture of these. The usual symptoms are a dry cough, often with sneezing, and a moderate eye and nostril discharge.

Dogs can be protected against this disease by special vaccines administered either by injection or, in some cases, as nasal drops.

Tummy problems

There are numerous causes for tummy troubles in a dog but if you are worried or the symptoms persist for longer than twelve hours, you should consult your veterinary surgeon. If your dog has a minor tummy upset, you could try feeding him some rice or pasta cooked with chicken, or some other bland meal.

COMMON SYMPTOMS
- **An affected dog may experience vomiting, diarrhoea, constipation**
- **There may be blood in the dog's droppings**
- **The dog may lose his appetite and refuse food**
- **Flatulence may be present**
- **The dog may eat or drink more than normal**
- **He may drink less than he normally does.**

Vomiting

Vomiting may be simple and transient due to either a mild infection (gastritis) of the stomach or to food poisoning. If severe, persistent or accompanied by other major signs, it can indicate serious conditions, such as distemper, infectious canine hepatitis, an intestinal obstruction, leptospirosis or a heavy worm infestation. In this case, seek veterinary attention urgently. The usual treatment for vomiting is to replace lost liquids (see diarrhoea below) and give the dog one to three teaspoons of Milk of Magnesia, depending on his size, once every three hours.

Diarrhoea

This may be nothing more than the result of a surfeit of liver or a mild bowel infection. However, diarrhoea can be more serious and profuse where important bacteria are present, in certain types of poisoning and in some allergies. Again, you should take your dog to the vet as soon as possible.

For mild cases of diarrhoea, cut out solid food, milk and fatty things. Give your dog fluids – best of all are glucose and water or some weak bouillon cube broth – little and often. Ice cubes can also be supplied for licking. Keep the animal warm and indoors.

Constipation

If your dog is constipated and is not passing any stools, it may be due to age, a faulty diet including too much chomped-up bone, or to an obstruction. Don't use castor oil on constipated dogs. Give liquid paraffin (a half to two tablespoons). Where an animal is otherwise well but you know that he is bunged up with something like bone which, after being crunched up, will set like cement in the bowels, you could get a suitable enema from the chemist.

Flatulence

'Windy' dogs may be the product of a faulty or changed diet. Often flatulence is associated with food that is too low in fibre although, paradoxically, too much fibre can have a similar effect. Generally, adjusting the dog's diet to one of high digestibility and low residue will do the trick. Adding bran to the dog's food will alleviate many cases.

Blood in the stools

This condition can arise from a variety of minor and major causes. It may be from nothing more than a splinter of bone scraping the rectal lining, or the cause may be more serious, such as the dangerous leptospiral infection. Your vet will be able to identify the cause and advise on suitable treatment.

Malabsorption

Some dogs with chronic diarrhoea (often rather fatty looking), associated with a strong appetite but loss of weight, are not able to digest or absorb their food normally. The causes include enzyme deficiency (liver or pancreas faults) or disease of the bowel walls.

The vet will employ a variety of tests to establish the cause and prescribe the appropriate therapy. Dogs deficient in pancreatic enzymes can be given pancreatic extract supplements with their food.

Polydipsia and polyphagia

Both of these conditions – polydipsia (drinking more than normal) and polyphagia (eating more than normal) – can be associated with diabetes, disease of the adrenal glands, kidney disease and other conditions. Careful examination of the patient by the vet, together with laboratory tests on blood and/or urine samples, is necessary to pinpoint the cause and thus lead to the correct treatment.

Salmonella infection

Salmonella is a type of bacterium that occurs in a wide variety of strains (serotypes) which may cause disease in, or be carried symptomlessly by, almost any species of animal. Sometimes salmonella can be found in the droppings of apparently normal healthy dogs. Dogs can contract salmonellosis by eating infected food, especially meat and eggs, or by coming into contact with rodents or their droppings, other infected dogs or, more rarely, reptiles or birds. The most common symptoms include diarrhoea (sometimes bloody), vomiting, stomach pain and even collapse, sometimes ending in death.

Diagnosis is confirmed by the vet sending away some samples for bacteriological culture and identification. The treatment is by means of specific antibiotics and fluid replacement. However, it is worth remembering that salmonella infection in animals may be transmissible to humans.

Parvovirus infection

This virus disease is spread via faeces. The incubation period is five to ten days and symptoms vary from sudden death in young pups, through severe vomiting, foul-smelling diarrhoea (often bloody), reduced appetite and depression to bouts of diarrhoea. Treatment includes replacing lost fluid, anti-vomiting and anti-diarrhoea drugs and antibiotics. Puppies can be vaccinated against parvovirus.

Acute abdomen

The sudden onset of severe pain, vomiting with or without diarrhoea and the collapse of the dog into shock is an emergency that necessitates immediate veterinary attention. The cause may be a powerful, rapidly-developing infection, obstruction of the intestine by a foreign body or a twist of the bowel itself, torsion (twisting) of the stomach, acute kidney, liver or uterine disease or poisoning. Successful treatment depends on quick diagnosis.

Urinary problems

Male dogs will urinate many times a day, in the course of a walk or a run in the garden. Bitches generally urinate less often. The usual signs of urinary disease are increased thirst and urination.

> **COMMON SYMPTOMS**
> • **Difficulty in passing urine**
> • **Urination is frequent**
> • **Blood is present in the dog's urine**
> • **More thirsty than usual.**

Types of urinary disease

If something is wrong with your dog's waterworks, see the vet. Inflammation of the bladder (cystitis), stones in the bladder and kidney disease are quite common and will need immediate professional advice. Whatever you do, don't withhold drinking water.

Leptospirosis

This is the most common disease of a dog's kidneys. Humans can be infected by contact with dogs who suffer from this. Symptoms can be acute with loss of appetite, depression, back pain, vomiting, thirst, foul breath and mouth ulcers, or more chronic with loss of weight and frequent urination. It can be diagnosed by blood and urine tests and treated with antibiotics. Vaccination is also available.

Cystitis

This inflammation of the bladder generally responds well to effective treatment with antibiotics, perhaps with medicines that alter the acidity of the urine and urinary sedatives.

Calculi

A diagnosis of stones (calculi) in the urinary system can be confirmed by your vet. In most cases, they are easily removed surgically under general anaesthetic.

Kidney disease

Kidney disease always needs careful management and supervision of the affected dog's diet. Chronic kidney disease patients can live to a ripe old age if the water, protein and mineral content of the diet are regulated, bacterial infection controlled, protein loss minimized and stress of any sort avoided. Prescription diets for chronic kidney cases are available from the veterinary surgeon and good pet shops.

Skeletal problems

The most common skeletal problems in dogs are arthritis and slipped disc. Arthritis is much more common in elderly dogs than in young ones.

COMMON SYMPTOMS
- **The dog may be lame**
- **He may experience difficulty getting up**
- **His gait may be stiff, slow or unusual**
- **There may be painful spots on bones or joints.**

Arthritis

This painful condition, to which Staffordshire Bull Terriers are relatively prone, may arise from the congenital weakness of certain joints, their over-use/excessive wear, injuries, infections and nutritional faults. Treatment is similar to that in humans, and your vet may well prescribe corticosteroids, non-steroidal anti-inflammatory drugs and various analgesics. At the first sign of your pet

having difficulty in moving, seek veterinary advice. Treatment is very effective but may have to be continued indefinitely.

Sometimes massages, perhaps with anti-inflammatory gels or creams, homoeopathic remedies and acupuncture can also afford relief and improved mobility in some dogs. If you are considering trying out alternative medical treatment, consult your vet first.

You should avoid taking your dog out in very cold or wet weather, and buy him a snug coat for outdoor use. Provide daily multivitamins and minerals following your vet's or the vitamin manufacturer's instructions and give elderly dogs, in particular, one to four capsules or teaspoons (depending on size) of halibut liver oil. Do not, in your enthusiasm for your pet, overdose the vitamins.

Painful joints

Arthritis can result in the thickening of the joint capsule, abnormal new bone forming round the joint edges, and wearing of the joint cartilage. The joint will be enlarged and painful and its movement is restricted. It tends to affect the shoulders, hips, elbows and stifles.

Obesity

Carrying excess weight can put extra strain on a dog's joints. Slim down an overweight dog by modifying his diet (reducing carbohydrates and fats), feeding special canned slimming rations, desisting from giving him sweet titbits, and increasing his exercise gradually. Your vet may run a slimming programme: expert guidance will be provided and your dog's progress will be monitored by regular weighing.

Slipped disc

The dog's adjacent spinal vertebrae are separated by discs shaped rather like draughts pieces, that act as shock absorbers when functioning correctly. With the passing of time, as dogs grow older, the discs lose their elasticity and become more brittle, less compressible and degenerated. Then, a sudden movement or trauma can cause a disc to 'burst' with the discharge of crunchy material that piles up against the spinal cord or a nerve root with the consequent rapid onset of symptoms. The disc itself does not actually 'slip' out of line with the spine. Staffordshire Bull Terriers are not particularly prone to 'slipped discs' which occur more commonly in breeds with long backs and short legs, such as Dachshunds and Pekingeses.

Symptoms and treatment

The signs of a slipped disc include sudden onset of neck or back pain, paralysis or weakness of the limbs, loss of sensation, limb spasms and loss of control of the bladder. Accurate diagnosis is aided by X-rays. Treatment is by means of medication (analgesics, sedatives, anti-inflammatory drugs and anabolic hormones) and, in some instances, surgery to relieve the pressure on nervous tissues. Good nursing by the owner of the dog under veterinary advice is essential for the animal's recovery.

Skin problems

There are many kinds of skin disease that can affect dogs, and their diagnosis needs examination and often sample analysis by the vet. If you suspect skin problems, seek expert advice.

> **COMMON SYMPTOMS**
> • **Thin or bald patches in the coat**
> • **Scratching and licking**
> • **Wet, dry or crusty sores.**

Healthy tips

• Feed a balanced diet with sufficient fats
• Never apply creams, powders or ointments without trimming back the hair. Let oxygen get to the inflamed area
• Groom your dog regularly to keep his skin and coat healthy.

Mange

This is caused by an invisible mite that burrows into the skin and can be seen as crusty, hairless sores. Fleas, lice and ticks also cause damage to a dog's coat (see page 104) but they live among the hairs on the surface of the dog's skin. If you see or suspect the presence of any of these skin parasites, you must obtain a specially formulated antiparasitic product from the pet shop, chemist or your vet and treat your dog immediately.

Powders are of little use against mange, and drugs in bath or aerosol form are more appropriate. Tough, deep forms of mange, such as demodectic mange to which Staffords with their short coats are rather susceptible and which is often complicated by the presence of secondary staphylococcal bacteria,may be treated by your veterinary surgeon using a combination of baths and drugs given by mouth.

As there are several different types of mange, you should ask the vet to advise you on the best method of treating your particular case. With all anti-parasite treatment of skin diseases, it is extremely important that you follow the instructions on the label of the preparation being used.

Ringworm

This subtle ailment may need diagnosis by ultra-violet light examination or fungus culture from a hair specimen. Special drugs, which are given by mouth or applied to the skin, are used for ringworm. Care must be taken to see that human contacts do not pick up the disease from the affected dog. Wash your hands thoroughly after handling a dog known to have ringworm.

Lumps and bumps

These may be abscesses, cysts or tumours and they may need surgical attention if they persist and grow larger. The earlier a growing lump is attended to, the simpler it is to eradicate, so you must consult your vet by the time it reaches cherry size.

Hot spots

Sudden, sore, wet 'hot spots' that develop in summer or autumn may be caused by an allergy to pollen and other substances. Use scissors to clip the hair over and round the affected area to a level with the skin, and apply liquid paraffin. Consult your vet as the dog may need anti-histamine or corticosteroid creams, injections or tablets. Although they look dramatic, hot spots are quickly settled by treatment.

Nursing a sick dog

In all your dog's ailments, mild or serious, you will normally have to be prepared to do something to look after his welfare, usually acting in the capacity of nurse. This will involve learning some essential nursing techniques, such as how to take the animal's temperature and administer tablets and liquid medicines.

Be confident

When you are treating a sick dog, it is very important to always adopt a confident and positive approach. Be prepared and have everything ready in advance before you undertake any of the following procedures. Your dog will be reassured by your calmness.

Taking the temperature

You cannot rely on the state of a dog's nose as an effective indicator of his temperature, good health or sickness. As with children, being able to take your pet's temperature with a thermometer can help you to decide whether or not to call the vet and can also assist him in diagnosing and treating what is wrong.

You should use an ordinary glass thermometer, which you can purchase at most pharmacies. For preference, it should have a stubby rather than a slim bulb, or, better still, you can invest in an unbreakable thermometer, although these are more expensive. Lubricate the thermometer with a little olive oil or petroleum jelly and insert it about 2.5cm (1in) into the dog's rectum. Once it is in place, hold the thermometer with the bulb angled against the rectal wall for good contact. After half a minute, remove it and read the thermometer.

A dog's normal temperature will be in the range of 38–38.6°C (101–101.6°F). Taking into account a slight rise for nervousness or excitement in some dogs, you can expect under such conditions to read up to 38.7°C (101.8°F) or even 38.8°C (102°F). Higher than that is abnormal. Shake down the mercury in the thermometer before use, and be sure to clean and disinfect the instrument afterwards.

Administering medicine

Try to avoid putting medicines into your dog's food or drink, as this can be a very imprecise method. However, for dogs that are really averse to pills and capsules, you can conceal them in tasty titbits, but you must check that the dog has swallowed them.

Tablets, pills or capsules

These should always be dropped into the 'V'-shaped groove at the back of the dog's mouth while holding it open, with one thumb pressed firmly against the hard roof of the dog's mouth.

Liquids

These should be given slowly, a little at a time, by the same method or direct into the lip pouch with the mouth closed. They can be squirted through a syringe.

Handling your dog

It is very useful to know how to handle and restrain your dog effectively during visits to the vet, especially if he gets anxious about being examined or may even behave aggressively.

Making a makeshift muzzle

A muzzle is essential when a nervous, possessive, aggressive or sensitive dog is in pain and has to be handled or examined. Make one with a length of bandage, string, nylon stocking or a tie to prevent you or the vet being bitten.

By carefully positioning the muzzle not too far back, you can still administer liquid medicine by pouring it into the gap between the lips behind the encircling band.

1 Tie a knot in the bandage and wrap it around the dog's muzzle.
2 Cross the ends of the bandage at the bottom under the jaw.
3 Bring the ends round to the back of the dog's head and tie firmly.

At the vet's

It is important to know how to handle your dog when you visit the vet's surgery. Although some dogs trot in happily and do not mind being examined, others can be nervous and may even panic. Get your dog used to going to the surgery from a very early age and make the experience pleasurable. Very large dogs are usually looked at on the floor, but the vet will want to examine small to medium dogs on the examination table and you will have to lift your dog up.

Lifting your dog

To avoid injury, not only to your dog but also to your back, always bend your knees when picking him up. Support his body properly with one hand on his chest between the front legs and the other below his rear.

1 When lifting a Stafford, bend your knees and place one hand securely under his rear and the other around his chest close to your body.

2 With your hand at the rear, taking most of the dog's weight and holding him securely, rise onto one knee, keeping your back straight.

3 Keep the dog in a secure position, holding him close to your body, and then rise to your feet, bringing him up to chest height.

First aid

First aid is the emergency care given to a dog suffering injury or illness of sudden onset. The aims of first aid are to keep the dog alive, avoid unnecessary suffering and prevent further injury.

Rules of first aid

- Always keep calm: if you panic, you will be unable to help the dog
- Contact a vet as soon as possible: advice given over the phone may be life-saving
- Avoid any injury to yourself: a distressed or injured dog may bite, so use a muzzle if necessary
- Control any haemorrhage: excessive blood loss can lead to severe shock and even death
- Maintain an airway: failure to breathe or obtain adequate oxygen can lead to brain damage or loss of life.

Common accidents and emergencies require you to have a basic knowledge of first aid. In emergencies, your priorities are to keep your dog comfortable until he can be examined by a vet. However, in many cases, there is important action you can do immediately to help preserve your dog's health and life.

Burns

These can be caused by very hot liquids or by contact with an electrical current or various types of caustic, acid or irritant liquid. You must act quickly.

Electrical burns

Most electrical burns are the result of a dog chewing a live flex or cable, so wires should always be hidden, particularly from puppies, and electrical devices unplugged after use. Biting live wires can cause burns to the inside of the lips and the gums but may, in the worst cases, result in shock, collapse and death.

Recommended action First, switch off the electricity before you handle the patient. Examine the insides of the mouth and apply cold water to any burnt areas. If the gums are whiter than normal or blue-tinged, shock may be present. You must seek veterinary advice.

Chemical burns

Burns can be caused by caustic chemicals, and you must seek veterinary attention if this happens.

Recommended action Wash the affected area of the coat with copious warm soapy water and then seek veterinary advice.

Scalding with a liquid

Hot water or oil spillage commonly occurs in the kitchen. Although the dog's coat affords him some insulating protection, the skin beneath may well be damaged with visible signs only emerging after several hours have passed in many cases.

Recommended action You must apply plenty of cold water immediately to the affected area and follow this by holding an ice pack on the burn – a bag of frozen peas is ideal. Then gently dry the burnt zone with mineral oil (liquid paraffin) and seek veterinary advice.

Poisoning

The house, the garden and the world outside contain a multitude of substances, both natural and artificial, that can poison a dog. If you suspect that your dog has been poisoned, you must contact your vet right away. Frequently some symptoms, such as vomiting, blood in the dog's stools or collapse, which owners may imagine to be the result of poisoning, are actually caused by other kinds of illness.

A dog may come into contact with poisonous chemicals through ingestion or by licking his coat when it is contaminated by a noxious substance. Canine inquisitiveness and the tendency to scavenge can lead dogs to eat or drink some strange materials. Sometimes owners will negligently give dangerous substances to their pets. Occasionally, poisonous gases or vapours are inhaled by animals.

Types of poison

All our homes contain highly poisonous compounds, including weedkillers, pesticides (rat, slug and insect killers), fungicides, disinfectants, car antifreeze, lead compounds, caustic cleaning fluids, paint thinners, creosote and excessive amounts of patent medicines, such as paracetamol and aspirin.

COMMON POISONS
- **Mouse and rat killer**
- **Sleeping tablets**
- **Carbon monoxide gas in faulty heaters and car exhausts**
- **Weedkillers**
- **Corrosive chemicals, such as acids, alkalis, bleach, carbolic acid, phenols, creosote and petroleum products**
- **Antifreeze**
- **Lead paint, solders, putty and fishing weights**
- **Slug pellets**
- **Insecticides**
- **Rodenticides (warfarin)**
- **Herbicides**
- **Illegal bird baits.**

You should be aware that poisoning can also be caused by certain plants (see below), insect stings (opposite) and the venom of snakes and toads.

Poisonous plants

Dangerous plants are found in most people's garden and they include the bulbs of many spring flowers, holly and mistletoe berries, the leaves and flowers leaves of yew, box and laurels, sweetpea, wisteria and bluebell seeds, and all parts of the columbine, hemlock, lily of the

---

COMMON SYMPTOMS
The symptoms of poisoning vary but they may be evident as:
- **Digestive upsets, especially vomiting and diarrhoea**
- **Difficulty in breathing**
- **Convulsions**
- **Uncoordinated movements or even coma.**
Note: If any of these occur in your dog and you suspect poisoning, you must ring the vet immediately.

---

valley and ivy. You should also be mindful of the fact that some fungi are as poisonous to dogs as they are to humans, as are the blue-green algae that sometimes bloom on garden ponds in hot weather. Keep your dog away from these plants.

Recommended action Determining which poison is involved can be quite difficult if you don't know what the dog has come into contact with. Professional diagnostic methods at the earliest opportunity are vital.

1 Look for any evidence of burning or blistering in the dog's mouth caused by corrosive poisons.
2 Flush out the mouth with warm water and let him drink water or milk.

Corrosive substances
1 Wipe clean the contaminated area with rags or paper tissues and cut off congealed masses of hair with scissors. Cooking oil or petroleum jelly will help soften paint and tar.
2 Wash thoroughly with dog or baby shampoo and rinse well. Don't use paint thinners, concentrated washing detergents, solvents or turpentine.

Recommended action If the poison has been swallowed recently (within one hour), try to make the dog vomit by giving him either a hazelnut-sized chunk of washing soda (sodium carbonate) or some English mustard powder (a level teaspoon in half a cup of water for a medium-sized dog, and pro rata). Then take him to the vet immediately.

Bee and wasp stings
Painful, but usually single and with no serious general effects, insect stings require little more than removal of the sting itself in the case of bee stings (wasps and hornets do not leave their stings behind) by means of tweezers and the application of antihistamine cream. Rarely, death can ensue if a dog is subject to a large number, perhaps hundreds, of stings. Stings can also be serious if the tongue or mouth are involved.

COMMON SYMPTOMS
- **The dog's throat will swell**
- **If he is allergic to the insect venom, he will go into severe shock.**

Recommended action If your dog goes into shock, he will need anti-shock therapy, such as intravenous fluids, adrenalin and antihistamine injections. Keep him warm and make sure that his breathing is unimpeded while you obtain veterinary attention.

Snake bites
Britain's only venomous snake, the common adder, may sometimes bite a dog who disturbs it.

COMMON SYMPTOMS
- **Two tiny slit-like punctures in the skin, which rapidly become surrounded by a zone of swollen reaction**
- **Trembling, salivating, vomiting and staggering**
- **The dog may then go into shock and collapse or even die.**

Recommended action You must take the dog straight to the vet for treatment with adder anti-venom – do not delay.

Bleeding

The appearance of blood anywhere on a dog's body necessitates immediate close inspection. A variety of accidents and some diseases may produce blood from the nostrils, eyes or ears or in the droppings or in vomited material. None of the above types of haemorrhage are usually suitable for first aid by the owner. All need veterinary attention, however, though the causes may often be trivial and ephemeral.

Bleeding from the body surface through wounds inflicted during fights, traffic accidents or other traumatic incidents can be copious, and this does require prompt first aid.

Recommended action The most important thing you can do is to apply pressure to the wound. Hand or finger pressure is always invaluable until a pad of gauze or cotton wool can be found. This should be soaked in cold water, placed on the wound and kept in place by constant firm pressure or, better still, a bandage. Take the dog to a veterinary surgery as quickly as possible. Do not waste any time applying antiseptic ointments or powders to a significantly bleeding wound.

Heat stroke

Every summer we read in the newspapers of cases of dogs dying from heat stroke as a result of the gross thoughtlessness and negligence of their owners. Just like babies and young children, dogs who are left in hot, poorly ventilated spaces, particularly cars, and sometimes without water, will overheat. Even on a warm day, don't leave your dog in the car.

> **COMMON SYMPTOMS**
> - Inability to control internal body temperature
> - As the latter rises, the dog will become distressed, pant rapidly and will quickly weaken
> - The dog's mouth will appear much redder than normal
> - Collapse, coma and even death can follow in a reasonably short space of time, so you must act quickly.

Recommended action Cooling the affected dog's body, particularly his head, by means of cold water baths, hosing and ice packs is essential. If the temperature-regulating mechanism in the brain has already been seriously damaged a fatal outcome may still ensue. Veterinary attention must be obtained immediately. Of course, by being a responsible and thoughtful owner, you can prevent such emergencies occurring.

Foreign bodies

Foreign bodies of various sorts (see below) can occur in different parts of a dog's anatomy and the treatment will vary according to the location.

In the eye

Foreign bodies in the eye will cause the dog to rub his head on the ground and paw at his eye. These must be treated as soon as possible

Recommended action Flood the affected eye with human-type eye drops or olive oil to float out the foreign body. Do not use tweezers close to the eyeball. If in doubt, take the dog to the vet.

In the ear

Plant seeds and grass awns are particularly likely to get into a dog's ears during summer walks. Their presence will cause itching and irritation. The dog will shake his head and scratch and paw at his ears.

Recommended action Pour some warm olive oil or other vegetable oil into the affected ear, filling it. The object may float to the surface and it can then be picked up easily with some tweezers. Deeper, embedded foreign bodies, however, will always require veterinary attention.

In the mouth

Pieces of bone or splinters of wood can become lodged in a dog's mouth. The offending object may be jammed between the left and right upper molars at the back of the mouth or between two adjacent teeth. Less commonly, an object, such as a small ball, gets stuck in a dog's throat. In all cases, he will show symptoms of distress, including pawing at the mouth, gagging, trying to retch or shaking his head.

Recommended action While someone assists you and holds the dog firmly, you should open his mouth and try to dislodge the foreign body with a spoon or some kitchen tongs. In those cases where the dog is having difficulty breathing and literally choking, try holding him upside down, massaging the throat and slapping his back. However, if this does not work and you cannot remove the object, you must seek veterinary help at once.

In the paws

Splinters of glass, thorns, particles of metal and even fragments of stone can penetrate the pads on a dog's paws or lodge in the skin between the toes. As a result, the dog limps and usually licks the affected paw.

Recommended action If the object is visible, you can remove it with tweezers. If not, because of being embedded, then bathe the foot two to three times daily in some warm water and salt (a teaspoon of salt to a cupful of water) until the foreign body emerges from the softened skin. If lameness persists for more than a day or two, seek veterinary attention as infection may set in.

Fish hooks

You must never attempt to pull out a fish hook, wherever it is. Instead, use pliers to cut the end of the fish hook and then push the barbed end out through the skin. If it looks sore, rub in antiseptic cream. If you are nervous about doing this, see the vet.

Useful information

Organizations

Association of Pet Behaviour Counsellors
PO Box 46
Worcester WR8 9YS
tel: 01386 751151
www.apbc.org.ok

British Veterinary Association
7 Mansfield Street
London W1M 0AT
tel: 020 7636 6541
www.bva.co.uk

DEFRA
Ergon House
c/o Nobel House
17 Smith Square
London SW1P 3JR
tel: 020 7238 6951
www.defra.gov.uk

The Kennel Club
1–5 Clarges Street
Piccadilly
London W1Y 8AB
tel: 0870 606 6750
www.thekennelclub.org.uk

Magazines

Dog World
www.dogworld.co.uk

Dogs Monthly
www.dogsmonthly.co.uk

Dogs Today
www.dogstodaymagazine.co.uk

Our Dogs
www.ourdogs.co.uk

Your Dog
www.yourdog.co.uk

Websites

Animal Health Trust
www.aht.org.uk

Dangerous Dogs Act 1991
www.opsi.gov.uk/ACTS.acts

National Dog Tattoo Register
www.dog-register.co.uk

Petlog
www.thekennelclub.org.uk/meet/petlog.html

Royal College of Veterinary Surgeons
www.rcvs.org.uk

Stafford rescues
www.staffordwelfare.com
www.eastangliansbtclub.co.uk/rescue.html
www.sbtrescue.org.uk/index.htm

Other rescue organizations
www.staffycross.org
www.oldies.org.uk
www.dogrescuenorfolk.com/index.htm
www.dogsos.co.uk
www.hoperescue.org.uk
www.nasatrust.co.uk
www.keithsrescuedogs.org
www.mutts-in-distress.org.uk

Staffordshire Bull Terriers UK
www.staffords.co.uk

Index